The
COLORADO PLATEAU

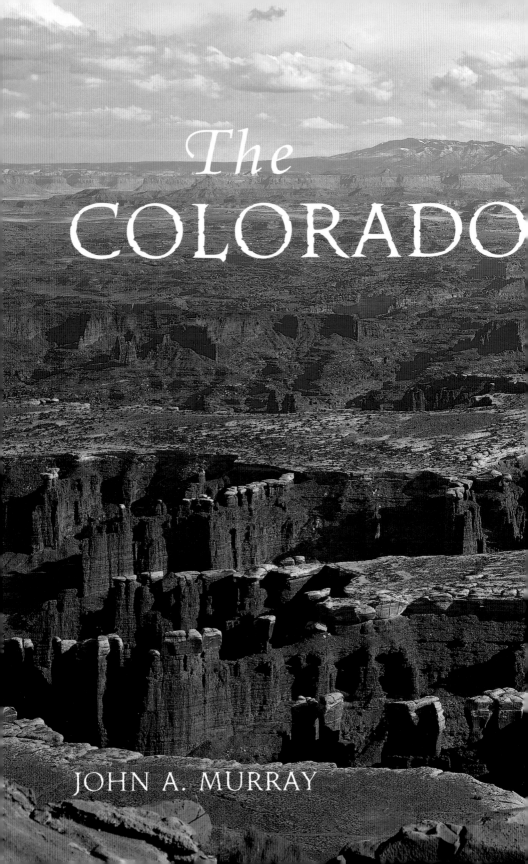

The
COLORADO

JOHN A. MURRAY

PLATEAU

A Complete Guide to the

National Parks and Monuments of

Southern Utah, Northern Arizona,

Western Colorado, and

Northwestern New Mexico

 Northland Publishing

for Terry Tempest Williams

❖

The text type was set in Minion
The display type was set in Minion, Centaur, and Pitchfork
Composed in the United States of America
Designed by Trina E. Stahl
Edited by Heath Lynn Silberfeld
Editorial direction by Erin Murphy and Tom Carpenter
Production supervised by Lisa Brownfield
Printed in Hong Kong by Midas Printing Limited

FIRST IMPRESSION
ISBN 0-87358-706-5

Library of Congress Cataloging-in-Publication Data
Murray, John A., date.
The Colorado Plateau : a complete guide to the national parks and monuments of southern Utah, northern Arizona, western Colorado, and northwestern New Mexico / John A. Murray.
p. cm.
Includes bibliographical references and index.
ISBN 0-87358-706-5
1. Colorado Plateau—Guidebooks. 2. National parks and reserves—Colorado Plateau—Guidebooks. I. Title.
F788.M89 1998
917.91'30453—dc21   97-31797

667/7.5M/3-98

TITLE SPREAD: Grandview Overlook, Canyonlands National Park
OPPOSITE: Lipan Point (South Rim), Grand Canyon National Park

❖

In the house of long life, there I wander.

In the house of happiness, there I wander.

Beauty before me, with it I wander.

Beauty behind me, with it I wander.

Beauty below me, with it I wander.

Beauty above me, with it I wander.

Beauty all around me, with it I wander.

In old age traveling, with it I wander.

On the beautiful trail I am, with it I wander.

Dawn Boy's song on entering White House, "Navajo Myths, Prayers, and Songs,"
University of California Publications in American Archaeology and Ethnology,
volume 5, number 2, Berkeley (1907)

Contents

PREFACE

❖

From the flat red sea of sand rose great rock mesas, generally Gothic in outline, resembling vast cathedrals. They were not crowded together in disorder, but placed in wide spaces, long vistas between. This plain might once have been an enormous city, all the smaller quarters destroyed by time, only the public buildings left.

WILLA CATHER, *The Professor's House* (1925)

If you have watched *She Wore a Yellow Ribbon,* or *The Greatest Story Ever Told,* or *Butch Cassidy and the Sundance Kid,* you have been transported, for a few hours, to the Colorado Plateau. If you have opened a magazine and admired the colorful and bizarre rock formations in a car advertisement, you have glimpsed the Colorado Plateau. If you have owned a mountain bike and wondered where the best mountain biking is, you have sooner or later become acquainted with the Colorado Plateau. If you have taken up the sport of river rafting, you have at some time during the first summer heard tantalizing rumors, amazing descriptions, impossible accounts, wistful campfire reminiscences of the Colorado Plateau. If you have wondered where the pollen-yellow, energy-rich uranium comes from that powers those glittering spiderlike probes we periodically dispatch on five-year missions to Jupiter, Saturn, and beyond, you have learned about the Colorado Plateau.

The Colorado Plateau, also known as the Painted Desert or the Slickrock Country, is unlike any other part of North America or, for that matter, the world. Where to begin? Let us start with a few preliminary facts. Here is the world's greatest collection of natural rock arches and bridges—in Arches National Park alone there are 300 of them. Here are more national parks and monuments than in any other region of the country, including the largest contiguous national parkland in the Lower 48. Here are canyons as deep as four Empire State Buildings stacked on top of each other and as wide from rim to rim as Manhattan Island is long. Here are collapsed salt domes into which a sprawling Midwestern mill town could disappear, exposed dinosaur tracks as plain as the day on which they were made, and the empty stone villages—hundreds of them—of vanished civilizations that flourished while Europe languished in the Dark Ages. Geologically, the region is defined by what the Colorado River and its tributaries have done, over millions of years, to a vast sedimentary rock formation that ranges from Dinosaur National Monument on the north to the Painted Desert on the south, from Mesa Verde on the east to the frontier of the Mojave Desert on the west. What the elements have done—water on rock, day by day, century after century— is to make, to create, to sculpt a myriad of canyons, reefs, mesas, spires, pinnacles, bridges, free-standing fins, dissected volcanic cores, deeply eroded lava flows, and delicately balanced rocks.

It is an enormous outdoor museum, a living gallery in which those Old World masters—earth, wind, water, and fire—continually practice, and refine, their craft.

Through it all flows that greatest of rivers in the American West, the Colorado. I have stood at the headwaters of the Colorado River in Rocky Mountain National Park, at a place called Kawuneechee Valley, and watched the speckled brook trout dart among the polished stones, and listened to the bull elk bugle in the aspen groves, and I have jumped the miniature channel and spent the day on higher slopes among the snowfields that are the river's ultimate source. Farther downstream, near Yuma, Arizona, I have walked beside the Colorado 70 miles from its outlet on the Gulf of California and thought of how much the watercourse resembles the Nile near Luxor and the Valley of the Kings, with the thick green border of date palm trees and orange groves, and the low-flying herons and cranes and cropdusters, and the sun-baked dune fields beyond. Nowhere along its entire 1,450-mile length is the Colorado River more beautiful, more muscular, more powerful than on the Colorado Plateau.

Nowhere.

Why?

Because here the river is at its maturity, in full career, halfway between birth and death, still running for the most part wild and free through a country that was old even when creatures the size of railroad cars roamed the earth. On the Colorado Plateau you can see a landscape that stretches a hundred miles from horizon to horizon, a distance so immense the curvature of the Earth is visible. Everything in sight has felt the touch of the river or one of its hard-working tributaries.

It is not enough, of course, to stand on the overlook and peer into this, or any, country. One must, or at least I must, walk into it, touch it, smell it, even spill some blood on it, courtesy of a yucca spine or cactus barb. That is what this book is all about—helping you to understand and explore this rich and varied landscape. Remarkably, you will find in venturing across the Colorado Plateau a country little changed since the first expedition of Major Powell in 1869. You can still stand on Grand View Point, Muley Overlook, the Goosenecks, or Lipan Point and see no work of man or woman as you take in a scene that covers thousands of square miles.

Never before has there been a greater need for places like the Colorado Plateau. One-third of the adult population is overweight. One in four adults suffers from chronic respiratory disease from degraded indoor air. The average adult watches twenty hours of television each week, time once spent exercising, gardening, reading, worshipping, and enjoying the outdoors. Many individuals now devote the majority of their time to the very machines—personal computers—that were meant to liberate them. A recent issue of *Scientific American* reported that of the nearly 100,000 articles indexed in *Psychological Abstracts* from 1967 to 1994, 88,320 dealt with depression, anxiety, or anger. Only 2,389 were concerned with happiness. What all of this says is that the American people really do need to get outside more often, both for the body and the spirit. A wonderful thing about the Colorado Plateau is that the season is long and mild. It may be five degrees below and snowing hard in Boston or raining for the twenty-third day in Seattle, but on the trails of Canyonlands National Park the spring sun will be shining brightly and the sego lilies will be blossoming as they have for the last several million years.

In the end, we know little of our condition. All around us are vast expanses of time and space. Truths and mysteries yet revealed deepen on every side. We are certain of little except that we are alive a short time. An eternity of perhaps nothing awaits us. Some cling to hopes of future good fortune. Others drift on legends of what might have been. I only know this. There are few things as beautiful as the shapes a desert river carves in the rock of a country, or the way a canyon rose holds its wine-colored blossom up toward the sun, or the sound of the wind against the rocks as you climb toward the summit of a solitary peak. To have been among these places is to have become acquainted with a happiness not often found elsewhere in the world.

A quartz crystal in its angular symmetry reveals the atomic structure of matter. In the same way do our acts of love, however small and seemingly insignificant, present an outward manifestation of ultimate nature. One could sit alone in the desert for thirty years, as with the early Christian fathers, and probably advance no further toward that elusive final truth. Love them, dear readers, these lost and lonely lands, and you will find that in the end what you get back is equal to what you give.

J.A.M.
Somewhere in the Devil's Garden
ARCHES NATIONAL PARK

INTRODUCTION

❖

Up from the sea, from the fogs and mists of the Atlantic,

the flat basin of the Mississippi, the plains of Kansas, and the

low divides of eastern Colorado! Up to the great stretches of

the Plateau Country where the sky is unending, the light unfailing,

and the clean air still blows over an unbroken wilderness!

JOHN VAN DYKE, *The Grand Canyon of the Colorado* (1920)

It is always helpful to know something of a country as you travel across, through, and eventually deeper into it. To know, for example, that a child's sandal you spot among the charred corncobs in a cliff dwelling near the San Juan River is 700 years old and should never be disturbed, or that the smooth dark rock you touch in the Inner Gorge is one-tenth the age of the universe and holds more wisdom than all the lecture halls on Earth, or that the smoky blue mountain range (the Henry Mountains) west of your eagle perch on the Green River overlook was the last mountain range named in the United States and that every May the loveliest wildflowers in the land brighten its slopes: pale white evening primrose, shooting star, and Indian Paintbrush.

And so I have written this introductory essay in that spirit of shared discovery. Think of it as an informal safari across various geological ages and human epochs, touching on matters of essential and common interest to all lovers of the Colorado Plateau.

HUMAN HISTORY

Every western city hell-bent for expansion

might ponder the history of Mesa Verde.

WALLACE STEGNER, *Where the Bluebird Sings*
to the Lemonade Springs (1994)

The Colorado Plateau was first seen by a European in 1540. In that year, there were no European settlements—none at all—on either coast of North America. It would be another quarter-century before

The Goosenecks on the San Juan River,
Glen Canyon National Recreation Area

the first doomed British colony was established at Roanoke, Virginia. Back in England, Henry VIII, desperate for a son to inherit the throne, would marry his fifth wife. His seven-year-old daughter Elizabeth, destined to become England's greatest monarch, could only watch, most likely in disbelief. The Vatican was about to establish the Jesuit order. Soon it would form the Inquisition. Michelangelo was the world's leading artist. The latest invention was the printing press. Copernicus had recently suggested that the Earth revolved around the sun. It would be only another seventy-six years before the Church forced Galileo to sign a document stating that the sun revolved around the Earth. The middle class, emerging from a thousand winters of feudalism, was just beginning to flex its muscles, primarily through the guilds, and this popular new faith called Protestantism. Across Europe, philosophers agreed that, of all forms of government, democracy—factions, corruption, rebellions, civil war, military coups—was the worst. By the end of the century a former stable boy from Stratford-on-Avon would be writing plays about the shortcomings of that other form of government: monarchy.

In the heart of the Colorado Plateau, a young Spanish lieutenant named Garcia Lopez de Cardenas was slowly making his way across the Tusayan or Hopi country, investigating rumors of handmade silver jewelry. It was slow going across a rocky dry country, week after disappointing week, with no maps and only the sun and the stars for guides. One hot July afternoon, half lost and searching as always for water, de Cardenas and his party found themselves approaching the rim of an extraordinarily prodigious canyon. But this was no ordinary prodigious canyon. It was of a scale that plainly dwarfed anything back in Spain or down in Mexico. It was a gulf in the Earth that made the explorers feel, as it does everyone, as insignificant as the atoms of Democritus. It was, de Cardenas later wrote, "a barranca [deep canyon] of a river, to which it was impossible to find a descent anywhere by beast or man, the barranca so buttressed by cliffs that it was hardly possible to see the river, which from above appeared like a mere arroyo."

For three days the explorers attempted to reach the distant Colorado, or red, river, before giving up and returning south.

As is customary in human affairs, many years—forty to be exact—passed before another of Spanish language and country visited the region again. The place, after all, had not much to recommend it. Certainly there was not the wealth of the Aztecs or Incas in the province, nor was there a prosperous human population to enslave or convert. There was just this vast canyon, the ramparts and cliffs of which had easily defied even the indefatigable conquistadors. With Arcadies like California and the Rio Grande Valley to excite the imagination, the high windy plateau was soon forgotten by the New World Europeans.

The scientific people believe that for at least ten thousand years prior to de Cardenas a succession of cultures inhabited the Colorado Plateau. Like all Native Americans, these individuals traced their ancestry to northeastern Asia. Generation after generation they drifted south into the Western Hemisphere, following the Pleistocene megafauna—mastodons, mammoths, steppe bison—that were slowly hunted into extinction. After many millennia, some subtle but significant changes began to take place among the human residents of the Plateau. For one thing, corn was introduced from Central America, which led to a less nomadic lifestyle. For another, families and clans began to build more permanent living structures and make pottery for food storage and preparation. Finally, around 700 A.D. the bow and arrow replaced the less efficient spear and atlatl (wooden spear-thrower) as the hunting weapon of choice.

During this period several cultural groups flowered in the American Southwest: the Hohokam of southern Arizona, the Mogollon of southwestern New Mexico, the Sinagua of the Verde Valley and Flagstaff area, and the Anasazi (Navajo for "the ancient ones"). Of these four, only the Anasazi inhabited the Colorado Plateau. During a brief golden age (1100 A.D. to 1300 A.D.) the Anasazi flourished. Their cliff houses and stone cities are still visible at such locations as Canyon de Chelly, Mesa Verde, Hovenweep, and

Anasazi rock art in southern Utah

Chaco. These distinctive dwellings were most often situated in alcoves above the canyon floors—protected spots that were shaded and cool in the summer, sun-washed and warm in the winter. They do not intrude upon the landscape as contemporary wood frame or brick houses do, for the homes of the Anasazi were built directly from the landscape—from sandstone and mud. Although we often pride ourselves on the accomplishments of our civilization, it remains to be seen whether our homes will be standing one thousand years from now.

Like the Hohokam and Mogollon, who lived to the south, the Anasazi cultivated corn and squash and hunted small game, especially rabbits and turkeys. At some locations, such as Chaco, the Anasazi built dams and ditches to direct the flow of water into cultivated fields. They also constructed roads between their cities. Much controversy surrounds the fate of the Anasazi, who disappeared suddenly around 1300 A.D. Popular scholarly theories include prolonged drought, overpopulation, environmental degradation, political or religious conflict, and the appearance of an aggressive new people. As with the decline of any human civilization, the truth probably involves a combination of all these factors. Many scientists believe the Anasazi did not die out but became the people we now call the Hopi.

Within a few centuries a new group appeared on the last wave of major immigration from the far north. These were the Navajo, who came from the Athabaskan tribes of Interior Alaska. During the six years I taught at the University of Alaska, I never felt far from home. Whenever my Athabaskan students spoke their native language in class—it sounded just like Navajo. And of course during the Second World War the Navajo language saved many an American life in the Pacific theater, as the Japanese were unable to break the "mysterious code" used by Allied forces. The Navajo language, like its ancient relative, Chinese, is a tonal language, and pitch helps to designate particular words. The language is fascinating. Navajo, for example, employs a grammatical fourth person that enables a person to refer to someone in the immediate vicinity without actually naming that person. Also, nouns are divided into "speakers" (humans) and "callers" (plants and animals). If you are driving across the Navajo Reservation, you might want to find the Navajo stations on the AM or FM band of your car radio—the Navajo language you hear, like any tonal language, has a beautiful musical quality.

The Navajo are today the second most populous Indian tribe in the United States, with a population around 220,000. The reservation in the center of the Four Corners Region sprawls over 18 million acres (roughly the size of South Carolina) in northwestern New Mexico, northeastern Arizona, and southeastern Utah. Across the reservation you will regularly see the eight-sided mud-and-log hogans of the Navajo, and you will often smell the sweet fragrance of pinyon and juniper cooking fires. The doorways of hogans always face east to receive the first rays of the rising sun. In Navajo culture every part of the hogan is sacred to the Navajo, and the interior and the surroundings must be kept clean and in good order. Great care is taken in choosing a building site and as a result hogans nearly always seem a natural part of the environment.

The tribe is famous for its songs, stories, and poems. In the Navajo view of nature the Earth should not be harmed—it is the source of human life. People must maintain themselves in harmony with the natural environment or take steps to restore that balance. Elders still teach the sacredness of wild animals and how each has its place in the natural community. Even mountains are considered sacred—Navajo Mountain, a high turtle-backed dome near Rainbow Bridge, is visible across the reservation and is considered a holy eminence by the Navajo. The symbol for life, nature, and fertility in Navajo culture is pollen—everywhere in their literature and crafts you will find wildflowers. Before leaving the reservation, Navajo sometimes scatter pollen on the boundary to ensure their safe return. Life on the reservation, with its rugged topography and extreme climate, though, has never been easy, and the dangers of nature are often personified in Navajo folklore, as in "The Rock Monster that Kicks People Off" and "The Tracking Bear" and "The Cutting Reed People."

The tribe acquired horses, cattle, sheep, and goats from the Spanish in the sixteenth century, and today livestock grazing is the

Navajo hogan in Canyon de Chelly National Monument

prevalent way of life on the reservation. Unfortunately, in such a fragile desert environment the livestock have had a pretty negative impact on the range. The effects of overgrazing are visible in the prevalence of yucca and prickly pear cactus where formerly there was grass, in shallow channels that have turned into deep arroyos, and in the desertification of semi-arid landscapes. Even with these changes, though, much of the reservation shows little sign of human presence, compared to most other parts of North America (Front Range Colorado, the Los Angeles Basin, anywhere in the Midwest, the Eastern seaboard, or south Florida).

The Navajo are known around the world for their sandpaintings, handwoven wool rugs, and silver and turquoise jewelry. The rugs are extraordinary in their complicated geometric designs and unusual natural-dye colors, particularly the earthtones. For example, a dark brown dye is made by boiling yarn in black walnut shells, a pale yellow ochre dye is produced by boiling yarn in sagebrush leaves and twigs, and a bright orange dye is created by boiling yarn in fresh sunflower petals. Some rugs depict ceremonial dances or domestic scenes. Others are wholly abstract or depict wild animals or landscapes. All of these rugs powerfully evoke the stark beauty and unique ambiance of the Navajo Reservation. A single Navajo rug hanging on a wall can fill an empty room with the sunny, life-filled spirit of the Southwest.

Other Native Americans inhabit the Colorado Plateau, including the Hopi, who live on a reservation inside the Navajo Nation, and the Southern Kaibab and Paiute, who live in northern Arizona and southern Utah around Fredonia and Kanab. Both the Hualapai and Havasupai occupy reservations that adjoin the Grand Canyon. The Ute—traditionally a mountain tribe of the Colorado Rockies—have a reservation near Cortez in southwestern Colorado, as do the Jicarilla Apache. The Ute are known for their intricate beadwork, and the nearby Hopi are renowned for their pottery and kachina dolls. The Ute, like the Navajo, have a number of important Anasazi cliff dwellings on their reservation and maintain these sites as tribal parks. All of these Colorado Plateau tribes have an often contentious relationship with the federal government over such issues as water rights; the killing of federally listed endangered species (such as the bald eagle for ceremonial feathers); legalized casino gambling; rampant poverty, poor schooling, housing, and health care; and law enforcement and jurisdiction (the reservations are regarded under the law as independent nations).

After de Cardenas left the Colorado Plateau in 1540, the Spanish rarely visited the area for two centuries. A major factor was the steady resistance of these resident Native Americans, particularly the Hopi, to any incursions or excursions on traditional tribal land. On July 29, 1776, two Franciscan fathers—Dominguez and Escalante— left Santa Fe in an effort to find a more northerly route to California. Their travels led them through what is today northwestern New Mexico, western Colorado (to Dinosaur National Monument), central Utah, what we now call the Kaibab Plateau, and across what is today the Navajo Nation. By the time they returned to Santa Fe, 2,000 miles and five months later, the weary pilgrims had completed a counterclockwise circumnavigation of the Colorado Plateau. What they had encountered was a land that was relatively fertile in places (southwestern Colorado) and absolutely inhospitable in others (the vicinity of what we call Page, Arizona). Based on their crude maps, a popular caravan route known as the Old Spanish Trail developed between settlements along the Rio Grande and outposts in southern California. The trail led northwest from Santa Fe to the vicinity of what is today Moab and then wandered across the Green River before turning south toward the Virgin River.

The first American to venture into the region was the irrepressible Jedediah Smith, who passed through southern and central Utah during his legendary walkabout of 1826. Next in the historical record is Captain John Charles Fremont, who barely touched the northernmost edges of the Plateau during his expedition of 1843–44 and left no significant records. By 1848, following the cessation of the Mexican War, interest in the region was growing. Plans were drawn to build a series of railroads from east to west, and as a result two of the Union Pacific railroad surveys explored portions of the Colorado Plateau—the Gunnison and Whipple expeditions of 1853. Both recommended, with good reason, that routes to the north and the south would be more advisable.

During the 1850s several Mormon explorers also ventured onto the Colorado Plateau, including the Mormon scout W. D. Huntington, who in October of 1854 led a party of twelve into the San Juan River country and discovered the ruins of Hovenweep Canyon. Huntington was followed by Jacob Hamlin, who discovered Monument Valley north of the Hopi lands. The last expeditions in this early frontier period were those of Lieutenant Joseph Ives, who reached the South Rim of the Grand Canyon in 1859 and crossed the Navajo country to Fort Defiance, and Captain John Macomb, who in the same year discovered the ruins of what is today Mesa Verde National Park.

A little matter known as the Civil War diverted attention from the Plateau for the next ten years.

We come now to the decades following the peace at Appomattox, when scientists from the newly formed United States Geological Survey invaded the farthest reaches of the West, including the Colorado Plateau. The first expedition was that of John Wesley Powell, a one-armed Civil War veteran and geology professor at Illinois Wesleyan College. On May 10, 1869—two weeks after completion of the Transcontinental Railroad—Powell and his entourage stepped from a Union Pacific railcar at Green River, Wyoming. Powell's dream was to descend the Green River by boat to its confluence with the Colorado River, and then follow the Colorado River through the heart of the Colorado Plateau, a distance of some 1,000 miles. Despite grave warnings from trappers and Indians, Powell succeeded in brilliant fashion and returned for further trips in 1870 and 1871. His 1874 book *The Exploration of the Colorado River and Its Canyons,* written primarily to garner Congressional support for scientific exploration in the West, is now considered a classic of exploration literature. Everywhere the book is filled with Powell's intense love for nature, which formed at least partially as a result of his Civil War experiences:

> *When he who has been chained by wounds to a hospital cot until his canvas tent seems like a dungeon cell, until the groans of those who lie about tortured with probe and knife are piled up, a weight of horror on his ears that he cannot throw off, cannot forget, and until the stench of festering wounds and anesthetic drugs has filled the air with its loathsome burden,—when he at last goes out into the open field, what a world he sees! How beautiful the sky, how bright the sunshine, what "floods of delirious music" pour from the throats of birds, how sweet the fragrance of earth and tree and blossom!*

Another eminent writer and explorer of this period was Clarence Dutton, who comprehensively studied the geology of the Four Corners region from 1875 through 1881. His books include *Report on the Geology of the High Plateaus of Utah* (1880), *The Physical Geology of the Grand Canyon* (1882), and *Tertiary History of the Grand Canon District* (1882). Despite the dry titles, these works are every bit as eloquent as anything by Thoreau, Burroughs, or Muir. Dutton wrote with authority and clarity of the plateau and canyon country, as in this luminous passage on the Vermillion Cliffs near Page, Arizona:

> *But as the sun declines there comes a revival. The half-tones at length appear, bringing into relief the component masses; the amphitheaters recede into suggestive distances; the salients silently advance toward us; the distorted lines range themselves into true perspective; the deformed curves come back to their proper sweep; the angles grow clean and sharp; and the whole cliff arouses from lethargy and erects itself in grandeur and power as if conscious of its majesty. Back also come the colors, and as the sun is about to sink they glow with an intense orange vermillion that seems to be an intrinsic luster emanating from the rocks themselves.*

No one has ever written better about the Colorado Plateau than Dutton, a fact later acknowledged by Pulitzer Prize–winning author Wallace Stegner when he wrote his doctoral dissertation on Clarence Dutton (later published in 1954 as *Beyond the Hundredth Meridian*).

There were other geological survey teams in this period, including the Hayden survey, the King survey, and the Wheeler Colorado River expedition. Accompanying Frederick Hayden, a medical doctor turned geologist, on many of his trips was the Civil War veteran William Henry Jackson, who captured the rugged beauty of the Plateau country in his large 8x10 negatives. Jackson worked extensively in the Four Corners area in 1875 and in 1877, especially in the ruins of Mesa Verde and across northwestern New Mexico. Equally important were the expeditions of Clarence King and George Wheeler, which included the veteran Civil War photographer Timothy O'Sullivan. In 1871 Wheeler explored the lower stretches of the Colorado River near Needles and ascended the river to the Colorado Plateau, including the Grand Canyon. So fine were the photographs that O'Sullivan later took on the Colorado Plateau that seventy years later, after visiting the White House Ruins

Old ranching homestead in Arches National Park

at Canyon de Chelly, Ansel Adams wrote, "I photographed the White House Ruins from almost the identical spot and time of the O'Sullivan picture! Can't wait until I see what I got" (letter to Beaumont and Nancy Newhall, October 26, 1941). These early photographers set the standards for those who followed.

Just as important as the photographers were the artists. Chief among these was Thomas Moran, quite possibly the best draftsman in the history of American art. An English-born resident of Philadelphia, Moran was an engraver by trade and, like his contemporary Alfred Bierstadt, had never ridden a horse before coming west. After accompanying Hayden on his expedition to Yellowstone in 1871, Moran was changed forever, both as a person and as an artist. His giant 7x12-foot painting, *The Grand Canyon of the Yellowstone,* was quickly purchased for the U.S. Capitol building. Two years later he accompanied the Powell survey of the Grand Canyon. Moran fell in love with the landscapes of the Colorado Plateau and painted *The Chasm of the Colorado,* which has been on display at the Smithsonian Institution for the last century. Moran eschewed mere photographic realism and strove to convey a vivid sense of place. In 1879 he declared, "I place no value upon literal transcripts from Nature. My general scope is not realistic; all my tendancies [*sic*] are toward idealization. . . . Topography in art is valueless."

By the 1890s the exploration of the Colorado Plateau had moved past the age of discovery. Events were proceeding rapidly across the West. The Mining Law had been passed, which to this day allows corporations to buy land for a few dollars an acre and then extract minerals—public property—for nothing. Ranchers were moving in and soon would be supported by the Taylor Grazing Act. President Grant, inspired by artist George Caitlin's dream of a "nation's park" on the old frontier, had designated Yellowstone National Park in 1872 and Presidents Harrison and Cleveland had begun the practice of establishing forest reserves, some of them on the Colorado Plateau. At the dawn of the twentieth century Theodore Roosevelt followed suit, and went even further in creating both the national monument system and the Forest Service. In 1908 he set aside Grand Canyon National Monument and the Grand Canyon Game Preserve (which later became the Kaibab National Forest and a favorite hunting ground of both Roosevelt and Western writer Zane Grey).

Two of the first professional writers to visit the Grand Canyon were John Muir and John Van Dyke. Muir, who is best known for his writings on California and Alaska, visited the Grand Canyon in 1902 and later that year published a lengthy essay on the canyon in *Century* magazine (a sort of *Outside* of the period). A few years later John Van Dyke, a professor of art history at Rutgers University, came for a more lengthy stay and was equally moved. His book *The Grand Canyon of the Colorado,* published in 1920, is one of the finest books ever written on the Grand Canyon. Van Dyke, like Muir, represented a new development in the national consciousness—an anti-frontier perspective bent not on exploitation but on preservation. A third important writer of this period was Willa Cather, whose novel *The Professor's House* (1925) includes a central story about the discovery of cliff dweller ruins in the Four Corners region and features some lovely descriptive passages.

Throughout the early decades of the twentieth century, new parks and monuments were being designated on the Colorado Plateau, including Mesa Verde (1906), Petrified Forest (1906), Natural Bridges (1908), Navajo (1909), Colorado (1911), Yucca House (1919), Zion (1919), Bryce Canyon (1923), Pipe Spring (1923), Arches (1929), Cedar Breaks (1933), and Capitol Reef (1937). With the designation of so many new national parks, tourism began to flourish. During the 1920s various dude ranches, trading posts, lodges, and private museums sprouted up on the Plateau. One of the best known was Harry Goulding's outpost in Monument Valley (the lodge still exists). It was Goulding who persuaded Hollywood cinematographer John Ford to come out for a visit. The future six-time Oscar winner was immediately struck by the big-screen possibilities of the dramatic monoliths and wide open country and filmed his cavalry trilogy in Monument Valley (*Fort Apache, She Wore a Yellow Ribbon,* and *Rio Grande*), as well as his masterpiece, *Wagon Master,* about the early Mormons. The country became synonymous with the acting style and screen presence of John Wayne and the frontier ethos and mythology his roles represented. Later films produced on the Plateau include *The Greatest Story Ever Told, Butch Cassidy and the Sundance Kid,* and *Raiders of the Lost Ark.*

During the Dust Bowl days of the 1930s and the lean war years of the 1940s the finest landscape photographers and artists of the age—Ansel Adams, Eliot Porter, Maynard Dixon, and Georgia O'Keeffe—often visited the Colorado Plateau. Their images helped to publicize the area and build an advocacy group in the same manner that the paintings of Moran and the photographs of O'Sullivan and Jackson had in earlier times. One of the funniest stories from this milieu regards a rafting trip made by Georgia O'Keeffe and Eliot Porter down the San Juan River. During the journey Eliot Porter found an unusually beautiful river stone. It was worn glassy smooth by the current and possessed striking colors. O'Keeffe asked Porter if she could have the stone to paint and he said no, having already hatched an amusing plan. A few months later, Porter invited O'Keeffe over for dinner at his home in Santa Fe and placed the stone in a conspicuous location. After O'Keeffe went home that night Porter and his wife observed that—sure enough—the stone had disappeared. According to her biographer, Roxanne Robinson, O'Keeffe later painted one of her most distinctive paintings using the stone.

Soon after the start of the Cold War, uranium was discovered on the Colorado Plateau, and there followed a frenzy of uranium mining. At all hours of the night and day there were helicopters and planes overhead, eager prospectors in Willy's jeeps with Geiger counters, ore trucks on the road, and distant explosions. Towns with strange names—Nucla, Uravan—appeared on the map. Mills were built, and people began to come down with various fatal diseases. Eventually the mining craze subsided as demand waned and ore prices fell. Despite the extensive mining, the Colorado Plateau was fortunate. Both the Great Basin Desert and the Mojave Desert to the

The Colorado River in Canyonlands National Park

west were used for above-ground nuclear testing, which is by any standard far worse than closed-shaft mining.

The fifties and sixties brought a small army of writers and activists to the Colorado Plateau—David Brower, Joseph Wood Krutch, Wallace Stegner, Colin Fletcher, and Edward Abbey. Abbey worked for three seasons in then Arches National Monument during the 1950s and subsequently wrote *Desert Solitaire* (1968), a book that reads like a long love letter to the Colorado Plateau. Equally important is Colin Fletcher's 1968 *The Man Who Walked Through Time,* which chronicles his 200-mile traverse from west to east along the Esplanade of the Grand Canyon, a feat never accomplished before or since. All of these writers were concerned with the salient environmental issues of the day, which included a plan to dam the Grand Canyon (which they successfully defeated), a plan to dam Glen

Canyon (which unfortunately succeeded despite their best efforts), a plan to dam the Green River in Dinosaur National Monument (which was also defeated), and a plan to create a new national park in the Canyonlands (which became a reality in 1964). During this period David Brower was particularly active as executive director of the Sierra Club; his large-format coffee-table books (such as *Navajo Wildlands* and *Time and the River Flowing*) were highly effective public education tools.

The 1980s and 1990s have seen the steady growth of tourism on the Colorado Plateau, the establishment of a sizeable new national monument (Grand Staircase-Escalante, 1996), and a protracted battle for the designation of new Utah wildlands (still unresolved at this time). In December 1995, during a Congressional deadlock over the budget, Grand Canyon National Park was closed for the first time in its history. Arizona Governor Fife Symington reportedly considered mobilizing National Guard troops to open the park (which would have led to the first confrontation of state and federal military forces since the Civil War). The following year Glen Canyon Dam released water for the first time since its construction, in a controlled attempt to restore natural water flow to the Colorado River downstream of the dam. That same summer an extensive forest fire (the Bridger's Knoll fire) burned on the North Rim of the Grand Canyon. More recently, there has been controversy in northern Arizona surrounding a proposed tourist development south of the Grand Canyon's South Rim.

Meanwhile, writers such as Terry Tempest Williams and Ann Zwinger carry on the fine literary traditions of John Van Dyke and Edward Abbey; landscape photographers such as Jeff Gnass and Jeff Garton pursue excellence with the same devotion as O'Sullivan and Adams; and painters such as Ed Mell and T. C. Cannon (sadly, now deceased; creator of such oil masterpieces as *Mom and Dad Have the Going Home to Shiprock Blues*) work with the same passion for the high desert as Thomas Moran and Maynard Dixon.

And the people keep coming by the millions, from spring break to late September, and beyond, and from nearly every country in the world.

It is a remarkable fact, and a testimony to American generosity and reverence for life, that the Colorado Plateau has remained largely unchanged since the time of Dominguez and Escalante. Everywhere there is growth, of course—the area becomes more popular every year—but the region is almost entirely public land, and so growth will forever be limited. So long as we support an unrestricted public domain as one of the cornerstones of our democracy and respect the biological integrity of the Plateau, the region will be safe. The only serious threat is the national debt, currently $6 trillion. In the years to come, it is likely that pressure will mount to sell the public lands—we have already seen proposals to that effect in the House. If such a liquidation of our most treasured assets were to occur, it would be the final disgrace in a Greek tragedy of national excess and political ineptitude.

When that defining moment in American history arrives, as it may, it might be well to recall the long conservation traditions of our country—most started ironically by Republican presidents—as well as the moving words of such Colorado Plateau writers as Edward Abbey:

> *The canyon country of southern Utah and northern Arizona—the Colorado Plateau—is something special. Something strange, marvelous, full of wonders. As far as I know there is no other region on earth much like it, or even remotely like it. Nowhere else have we had this lucky combination of vast sedimentary rock formations exposed to a desert climate, a great plateau carved by major rivers—the Green, the San Juan, the Colorado—into such a surreal land of form and color. . . . It is a regional, national and international treasure too valuable to be sacrificed for temporary gain, too rare to be withheld from our children. (From "Come On In" in* The Journey Home*)*

NATURAL HISTORY

Those who have long and carefully studied the Grand Canyon

of the Colorado do not hesitate for a moment to pronounce it by far the

most sublime of all earthly spectacles.

CLARENCE DUTTON, *Tertiary History of the Grand Canon District* (1882)

A basic knowledge of geology is indispensable when visiting the Colorado Plateau. The region is a veritable textbook of erosional geology, and with a little information much sense can be made of the landscape. All three of the great families of rock are found here—sedimentary (formed from layered deposits), metamorphic (created under pressure), and igneous (volcanic)—as are surface features found throughout the solar system, from the outback of Monument Valley to the uplands of Mars to the moons of the gas planets. During the 1960s the Apollo astronauts trained among the cratered and eroded landscapes of the Colorado Plateau, learning rock identification and landform recognition, before voyaging to the moon. One can imagine the same will occur in the future as astronauts who are now plying the Internet in junior high school prepare for missions to Mars.

For the time being, the Plateau is the single best place on Earth to learn about geology—how folds and faults alter the landscape (the Waterpocket Fold in Capitol Reef National Park, the Hurricane Fault near St. George, Utah) and the powerful erosional forces that cause the slickrock that is synonymous with the Colorado Plateau (Arches National Park, in particular). Four major rivers—the Colorado, San Juan, Green, and Dolores—carve the great plateau in their wide meanderings, exposing layers that range from the Cretaceous (most recent) to the Jurassic (the age of dinosaurs) to the Cambrian (earliest). Everywhere is the sort of scenery Bruce Springsteen had in mind when he wrote that song "Badlands." But it is a beautiful badlands, and the Plateau grows on you over time, until all other earthly scenery seems poor and dull by comparison.

The geology of the Grand Canyon, which is a microcosm of the Colorado Plateau, is an excellent place to start. It is a story so simple that any second-grader can comprehend it. What we have is a plateau that has been eroded by a river. That is all. No serried shield volcanoes, no active glacial sheets, no clashing tectonic plates or complex intercontinental faulting. Just water and rock. Think of the stairs from your living room to your basement. In the Grand Canyon we have the same thing: a series of benches, each representing a segment of history, all dropping progressively toward the river.

Run a garden hose over a sandbox and you have the same effect.

At the canyon rims we have the most recent layers. These top sediments are called Kaibab limestone. They range from 50 million to 250 million years in age. Observe one of these rock outcrops and you will be astonished at the marine fossils. There are crinoids as fine as the beads on a Navajo necklace, and mollusks swirled like miniature turbans, and delicate honeycomb sea fans, and tight bundles of stinging coral—all mixed together in the rock-hard sea bottom in which they once quietly died, a quarter of a billion years ago.

Beneath the Kaibab limestone is the Toroweap formation, a 300-foot tan-colored ledge that takes us back another ten million years—more mollusks and corals. Below the Toroweap formation is one of

Coconino limestone on the North Rim of the Grand Canyon

the most distinctive bands of color in the Grand Canyon—the bright white Coconino sandstone. As with the previous two layers, this one averages 300 feet in height and is as steep as the side of an office building. Hiking trails must find breaks in the Coconino to descend lower into the salmon-colored Hermit shale (280 million years old) and the Supai Group (300 million years old). Both the Hermit and Supai layers were formed not by seas but by swamps and lagoons, hence the fossils are mostly of primitive plants.

Once you reach the Supai Group, you can rest for awhile. For one thing, this layer is 600 to 700 feet in depth. For another, it corresponds with the Esplanade, the rolling pinyon and juniper middle ground of the canyon. It is on the Esplanade that Colin Fletcher made most of his fabled walk through the canyon. It is also on the Esplanade that most hikers look up—and wonder if they can make it.

Below the Esplanade we encounter a major problem—the Redwall limestone. Next to the band of white Coconino sandstone near the top, the Redwall is the most distinctive feature in the canyon. The Redwall ranges in height from 400 to 650 feet and in age from 330 to 350 million years. Like the others, it is vertical. As in straight up and down. Breaks in the Redwall are few and far between,

The Esplanade near Bridger's Knoll, Grand Canyon National Park and all trails in the canyon must contend with this rather effective barrier to travel. The Redwall limestone up close is a fine-grained stone containing all sorts of marine life—crinoids, brachiopods, bryozoans—native to shallow warm seas. The Redwall is actually gray but has been stained by runoff from the reddish-colored Hermit shale and Supai Group on the slopes above.

Four geological layers follow the massive Redwall, each older than the last: the Temple Butte limestone (reddish-purple), the Muave limestone (mottled gray), the Bright Angel shale (greenish), and the Tapeats sandstone (reddish-brown). By the time we reach the Tapeats sandstone, the rock is from what scientists call the Early Cambrian Age—about half a billion years old. At the lower levels, beginning with the Bright Angel shale, we find fossils of trilobites and worms—two of the oldest life-forms.

Below the Bright Angel shale we have the basement of time—the Grand Canyon Supergroup (the last 500 feet of rock to the river). These consist of truly ancient formations—Vishnu schist and pink granite—that range in age to 1.7 billion years. Considering that the solar system was only formed around 4.5 billion years ago, these rocks are at least one-third the age of the planet. Once the Vishnu schist was shale and basalt, but under tremendous heat and pressure the rocks crystallized into the dense and beautiful stone river rafters and canyon hikers now photograph. Touch one of these stones and you are touching time itself, something that existed before the Cambrian explosion created multicelled organisms, something that existed when one-celled life-forms trafficked in the tides of the moon. Who would have thought back then that from those swarming amoebas would one day evolve a creature that would guide a spacecraft to a gentle landing on the moon, discover the energy that powers the stars, and unlock the secrets of the DNA at the core of carbon-based life?

Speaking of DNA, there is a lot of it on the Colorado Plateau. And it takes the form of both plants and animals. Both are found in distinct communities, which are roughly distributed by altitude. At the lowest levels of the canyons we have a desert environment virtually indistinguishable from the Sonoran desert of southern Arizona. All that is lacking are the large arboreal cacti—saguaro and organ pipe. Everything else in the Sonoran is here: barrel cactus, ocotillo, brittlebush, hedgehog cactus, beavertail cactus. Close to the rivers, or any body of water on the Plateau, we have what is called the riparian habitat—cottonwoods and willows, reeds and cattails, leopard frogs and green moss, slow-moving warm-water fish. You will notice tamarisk on the sandbars—that is an introduced or exotic species originally from the Mideast. On the Dolores River in southwestern Colorado we now have river otters, recently restored in the canyon by the state of Colorado and adjusting well, according to biologist Tom Beck, who is managing the program from his kayak (the perfect job).

Ocotillo and brittlebush in Havasu Canyon, Grand Canyon

Above the Sonoran we have desert scrub—creosote bush, blackbrush, mesquite, sage, yucca, and prickly pear. Life is hard here, and water is often far away. The habitat is sun-baked in the summer and wind-blasted in the winter, and there are few if any trees. Scorpions and centipedes love it, as well as rattlesnakes and rodents, but little else. Most animals march quickly through the habitat on their way to somewhere else, and usually at night: bighorn sheep, ringtail cats, coyotes, and members of the always numerous rodent tribe. Just above the desert scrub, at around 3,000 feet in altitude, we begin to encounter the pinyon-juniper community. This habitat is, despite appearances, one of the most productive in the Southwest. How so? Both the juniper and the pinyon pine produce edible food—berries and nuts, respectively. There are also scrub oaks scattered here and there, and in good years the trees produce acorns, which are consumed by everything from squirrels to foxes to bears. Cliff rose, which in places forms small forests, is edible to the deer. Some of the densest mule deer populations in the West are found in the pinyon-juniper zone, and the turkey hunting is often superb (as the Anasazi well knew).

Mule deer were at the center of one of the greatest environmental disasters on the Colorado Plateau. It occurred on what is now the Kaibab National Forest on the North Rim of the Grand Canyon in the 1910s and -20s. In the bad old days, predators were considered bad (useless, without a functional purpose in nature) and prey were considered good (by the sport hunters who then dominated environmental policy). As a result, a decision was made by land managers to completely exterminate all predators (coyotes, wolves, mountain

lions, bears, raptors) on the Kaibab Plateau. Why? To build a huge trophy population of mule deer for the hunters. The effect could have been predicted by any freshman biology student—a herd that numbered 4,000 in 1900 exploded to around 100,000 by 1924, and then collapsed after consuming all available food. Over 80,000 deer died in the period from 1924 to 1930, before reaching

Bighorn sheep horn on rock

a population of around 10,000. Today a robust mountain lion population and carefully controlled hunting keep the deer populations in check (restored gray wolves would also help).

Above the pinyon, juniper, and oak, we have the ponderosa pine forests. These are particularly evident on the North Rim of the Grand Canyon above 8,000 feet and at higher elevations on the South Rim (west of Lipan Point on the South Rim road). Ponderosa pines are the most important commercial tree in the Southwest and are still actively harvested from the Kaibab National Forest. In the ponderosa forests are clearings with scrub oak, mountain mahogany, and cliff rose, as well as some grass meadows, which help to support populations of deer and elk. Wild turkeys are numerous, as are the tufted-ear Kaibab squirrels.

Beavertail cactus in bloom

At the highest elevations (over 9,500 feet) of the La Sal, Abajo, and Henry Mountains and on the Aquarius Plateau you will find forests of spruce and fir identical to those found in the far north of Canada. Aspen are plentiful, especially on the Aquarius Plateau. In autumn, the changing colors of the aspen can be spectacular. Deer and elk are abundant, as are black bear, bobcat, and coyote. Raptors are often seen, especially hawks and eagles. Although not often associated with the dry and rocky Colorado Plateau, such high, cool forests, resulting from heavy snowfall in the winter months, are actually quite widespread in the region. Their runoff helps to keep lower areas alive during the often brutal summer months.

There are many other interesting habitat areas in the Colorado Plateau. Potholes, for example, are semi-permanent tanks or pools that formed in eroded areas of the slickrock. Some attain such size as to accumulate sand, which in turns enables aquatic plants to root. After that, various aquatic animals take up residence, from desert shrimp to frogs and salamanders. At dusk and at dawn these watering holes are more popular with the local wildlife—rock doves, rabbits, rattlesnakes—than an isolated bar in a dry country. A whole book could be written on a pothole.

Hanging gardens, which form near seeps on canyon walls, are another of my favorite microsites on the Plateau. Such wet alcoves can harbor an astonishing assemblage of wildflowers. Some of the most accessible are in the canyon of the Virgin River in Zion National Park, where each summer red monkeyflower, orchids, bluebells, and golden columbine hang by the hundreds among the ferns and mosses. Somehow or another, poison ivy has also begun to make its presence known in such locales.

In both Canyonlands and Arches National Parks, you will find cryptobiotic soil, which is an ecosystem unique to the Colorado Plateau. In areas where there is not enough moisture to foster a grass covering, the fine powdery soil adopts microscopic life-forms. These in turn bind together to create a dark living crust that holds the soil in place. This crust is very fragile and, once broken, results in a degraded surface, which accelerates wind and water erosion. It is important to avoid disturbing these delicate crusts whenever possible—the soil is quite literally alive. I always try to walk on slickrock and, when crossing cryptobiotic areas, step on stones and deadfall as much as possible.

Endangered or rare species on the Plateau include the Colorado cutthroat trout, the Colorado River humpback chub, the Virgin River spinedace, the Coral Pink Sand Dunes tiger beetle, the Southwest willow flycatcher (a bird), the Kanab amber snail, the desert tortoise, the black-footed ferret, the Great Basin prairie dog, the desert bighorn sheep in some canyon areas, and the California condor. Beginning in 1996, the United States Fish and Wildlife Service began releasing captive-bred California condors in the Paria Canyon-Vermillion Cliffs Wilderness Area west of Page, Arizona. The last confirmed sighting of a condor in northern Arizona was in 1924 near Flagstaff. Researchers hope that the outstanding cliff sites available in the area will provide a suitable habitat for the big scavengers (condors do not kill their food but feed on animals other predators have killed). In the past the major sources of mortality for condors were powerlines, poaching, and illegally poisoned carcasses. With any luck, these amazing survivors of the Ice Age will make this remote area their permanent home.

❖

It increases and spreads

In the middle of the wide field

The white corn, it increases and spreads

Good and everlasting one, it increases and spreads.

Navajo Growth Song

So there you have it. The Colorado Plateau. A place to contemplate the mystery at the heart of a juniper seed, to ponder the blue flashes of lightning over Monument Valley, to study the thread of a river at the bottom of a mile-deep canyon, to note the whorls in a fingerprint that were pressed into the mud of a stone house 700 years ago, to befriend a raven and wander in the desert until you leave not the tracks of a man or a woman but the tracks of a deer or, in my case, a coyote. A place to wonder, at midnight on Grand View Point, how it is you came to occupy this body, this time, this planet, you, this mortal thing comprised of river clay and a hundred contradictions and yet somehow blessed with the grace of a canyon waterfall and given the light of a distant star.

❖

The Colorado Plateau abounds with archaeological, camping, hiking, and photography opportunities. Throughout this book, the following symbols designate places of especially significant or unique opportunities for these activities.

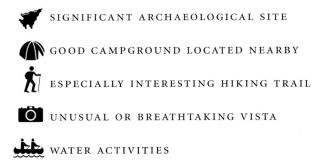

SIGNIFICANT ARCHAEOLOGICAL SITE

GOOD CAMPGROUND LOCATED NEARBY

ESPECIALLY INTERESTING HIKING TRAIL

UNUSUAL OR BREATHTAKING VISTA

WATER ACTIVITIES

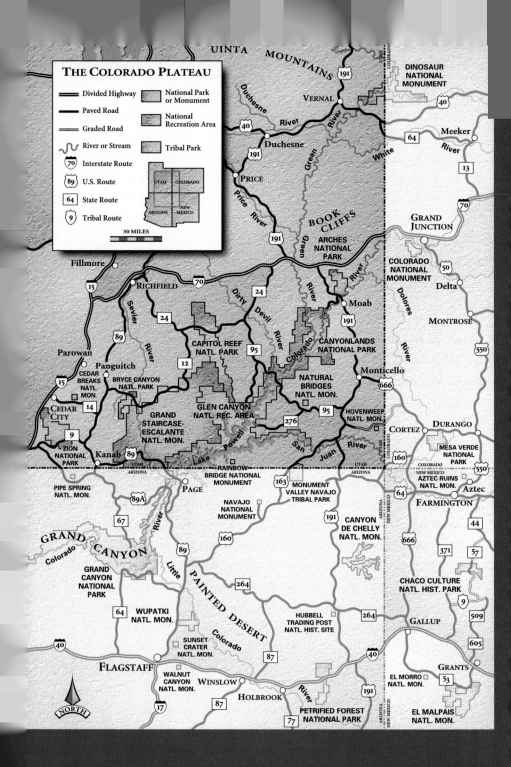

THE COLORADO PLATEAU

- ═══ Divided Highway
- ── Paved Road
- ══ Graded Road
- ∿ River or Stream
- (70) Interstate Route
- (89) U.S. Route
- [64] State Route
- (9) Tribal Route

National Park or Monument

National Recreation Area

Tribal Park

30 MILES

UTAH | COLORADO
ARIZONA | NEW MEXICO

UINTA MOUNTAINS

DINOSAUR NATIONAL MONUMENT

VERNAL

Duchesne River

40

Meeker

64

River

13

Duchesne

191

PRICE

Price River

191

GRAND JUNCTION

BOOK CLIFFS

70

ARCHES NATIONAL PARK

COLORADO NATIONAL MONUMENT

50

Delta

Fillmore

RICHFIELD

70

24

Moab

191

MONTROSE

550

Parowan

89

Sevier River

24

CAPITOL REEF NATL. PARK

95

CANYONLANDS NATIONAL PARK

Monticello

666

Panguitch

CEDAR BREAKS NATL. MON.

12

BRYCE CANYON NATL. PARK

GLEN CANYON NATL. REC. AREA

NATURAL BRIDGES NATL. MON.

95

HOVENWEEP NATL. MON.

Cortez

DURANGO

CEDAR CITY

14

GRAND STAIRCASE-ESCALANTE NATL. MON.

276

160

MESA VERDE NATIONAL PARK

9

ZION NATIONAL PARK

Kanab

89

Lake Powell

San Juan River

AZTEC RUINS NATL. MON.

Aztec

550

PIPE SPRING NATL. MON.

RAINBOW BRIDGE NATIONAL MONUMENT

163

MONUMENT VALLEY NAVAJO TRIBAL PARK

64

FARMINGTON

89A

PAGE

NAVAJO NATIONAL MONUMENT

67

GRAND CANYON

Colorado River

89

160

191

CANYON DE CHELLY NATL. MON.

44

666

371

57

GRAND CANYON NATIONAL PARK

Little Colorado River

PAINTED DESERT

264

CHACO CULTURE NATL. HIST. PARK

9

64

WUPATKI NATL. MON.

HUBBELL TRADING POST NATL. HIST. SITE

264

GALLUP

509

40

SUNSET CRATER NATL. MON.

87

605

FLAGSTAFF

WALNUT CANYON NATL. MON.

WINSLOW

HOLBROOK

River

GRANTS

EL MORRO NATL. MON.

53

17

87

PETRIFIED FOREST NATIONAL PARK

191

77

EL MALPAIS NATL. MON.

NORTH

OPPOSITE: Slickrock in Natural Bridges National Monument

SOUTHERN UTAH

THE GEOGRAPHY OF HOPE:

ARCHES NATIONAL PARK

❖

A weird, lovely, fantastic object out of nature like

Delicate Arch has the curious ability to remind us—like rock

and sunlight and wind and wilderness—that out there is a

different world, older and greater and deeper by far than ours.

EDWARD ABBEY, *Desert Solitaire* (1968)

*A*rches National Park contains the greatest density of natural arches in the world—over 300. There are arches barely large enough to squirm through and arches that would tower over a fifteen-story office building. There are double arches and delicate arches and tunnel arches. There are arches that look as though they might collapse in five minutes and arches that will still be standing when the human race has met its ultimate fate. There are arches just beginning to form and arches that began forming when our ancestors were still chipping points in Olduvai Gorge. There are arches the color of mountain lions, and arches the color of mariposa lilies in the shade. There are arches of nearly every tone on Earth, depending on the position of the sun, or the stars, or whatever clouds are passing through.

Just before sunrise, when the rocks emerge from the darkness, they begin to change color or, rather, take on color. Grays become gold, shadows assume the multitudinous hues of the spectrum. At noon they are the brightest. During a thunderstorm they are wet and sullen looking, and the rocks wear the snow well. They seem not to care about the people who swarm like ants around them, take their photographs, and leave. They seem to belong to another world. In fact, they are portals to another world. Step through, or beneath them, and you will be forever changed. The rain whistles through them and becomes snowflakes. Rock doves fly through them and become red-tailed hawks. Old men and women, standing in

Delicate Arch, Arches National Park

their portals, become as carefree and happy as children again, and children, touching the smooth stones, speak with the wisdom of the ages. They are places of magic and wonder.

In olden days the Indians came here because of the chalcedony, a type of quartz that makes an excellent arrowhead or spearhead. They camped down by the Colorado River and hiked up the side canyons and dry washes into the arches country where they found the raw materials to make their weapons. Along the way they often stopped to draw pictures or make handprints on the rock, pictographs visible to this day. Many years passed. After the Civil War a disabled veteran named John Wolfe came out and lived with his son for twenty years—their mouse-infested cabin can still be seen near the start of the trail to Delicate Arch. In 1929 the federal government declared the area a national monument—no one else knew what to do with it. Later (1971) it was given full national park status (about the time the price of uranium ore began to drop and Moab was looking for an economic boost). The only other history of note was made by Edward Abbey, the writer who worked as a ranger-naturalist in the park (then monument) for three years in the 1950s. His book— *Desert Solitaire* (1968)—is now ranked by scholars as one of the great works of American literature. Anyone contemplating a visit to Arches National Park should familiarize themselves with Abbey's masterpiece, which captures the "essence of the riddle of the paradox" of the beautiful canyon country. It is the ideal book to read either before a visit (anticipation is half the pleasure) or afterward (to remind one of the sweet beauty sadly left behind).

There are many excellent roads in the national park system. One thinks of the 90-mile dirt track that bisects the northern range of Denali National Park, on which I puttered in my Subaru every summer for six years, looking for grizzlies to shoot (with a camera). And there is U.S. 89 as it transits through Grand Teton National Park, with that sublime vertical landscape out of Bierstadt looming to the west. And there are others: U.S. 101 on the outer coast of Olympic National Park, Trail Ridge Road in Rocky Mountain National Park,

Park Avenue, Arches National Park

the Puerto Blanco road in Organ Pipe Cactus National Monument, the south rim of the Grand Canyon, and the Newfound Gap road through the Smokies. For my money, I'll choose the 28-mile black-top from the Arches National Park entrance to the Devil's Garden, and back. It was here I first fell in love with the desert, first began this great romance that has outlived six presidents, two wives, and four Superbowl blowouts by the Denver Broncos.

The road begins humbly enough, just beyond the perpetually crowded visitor's center, climbing a steep wall of massively fractured sandstone. RVs have been known to overheat on this stretch, particularly on a hot July afternoon. Soon it gets better. Up the road 1 mile is the parking lot to South Park Avenue. Pull over. Grab the camera and the kids. You are about to view one of the most stunning formations on the Colorado Plateau. These huge slabs—called "fins" by the geologists—are highly resistant chunks of Entrada sandstone. Also note the cryptobiotic soil and remember to avoid walking on such soil. The best spot for a photograph is dead center on the trail about 100 feet north of the parking lot—other views can be had farther down the trail, among the junipers in the wash, but they are less dramatic.

Next stop—just .5 mile farther—is the La Sal Mountains Overlook. Out beyond the blackbrush, prickly pear cactus, and spiked yucca are the lovely La Sal Mountains (Mount Tukunikivats is 12,721 high). If it is June, the peaks will still be wearing quite a bit of snow. If it is August, the snow will be pretty much gone from the summits. Like most of the mountain ranges in the Colorado Plateau, the La Sals are "laccoliths," formed when enormous domes of molten igneous rock pushed upward through the sedimentary rock and then eroded to reveal the indefatigable crystalline cores.

A mile farther are the Courthouse Towers—monoliths that evoke the free-standing formations of Monument Valley—and Courthouse Wash (good place for a hike). If it is a summer after a wet spring, you will notice that the junipers are literally covered with blue-colored berries—these berries are an important food source for the local wildlife. A mile and a half past Courthouse Towers is a vast stretch of petrified sand dunes dating to the Jurassic Period (age of dinosaurs)—they present the very picture of the sort of beautiful desolation that the Colorado Plateau is famous for. Another 3 miles down the road brings us to Balanced Rock—a sizeable boulder perched precariously on a stem of Entrada sandstone (the boulder is nearly 60 feet in diameter). If you placed that rock on one side of a pair of scales and shoveled all the injustices perpetrated against Native Americans onto the other, the scales would still not tip one millimeter from the latter to the former.

Just past Balanced Rock there is a turnoff to the south. Take it. You are entering what park managers call "The Windows Section." Here are some of the most fantastic arches in the park, or anywhere on Earth. These include Cove Arch, Turret Arch, Double Arch, and the North and South Windows, which provide panoramas of the Colorado River Valley and the La Sal Mountains to the south. Stop at each turnout in sequence and admire the local rings of stone for as long as you wish—the longer you watch them, as with anything, the more you will see. Like all the arches in the park, these were formed by a geological process known as exfoliation—the peeling off of layers of rock as a result of freezing and thawing. Like any great work of art, their creation took a long time, but the final product is, you have to admit, worth the wait.

Two and one-half miles beyond the turnoff to the Windows is the road to the Delicate Arch trailhead. As you have probably noticed, the license plates in Utah have the Delicate Arch on them, and for good reason. It is the most spectacular arch in the land. The trail to Delicate Arch, which I have trod many times with countless other pilgrims, is about 3 miles, round-trip. It does not seem very far on a cool spring morning, but it is insufferable on a searing summer afternoon (the trail is almost entirely over naked rock). Be certain to take enough water so that you can linger and admire the view. Sometimes people walk over to the base of the arch. I would not recommend this, for if you slip it is a long way down and the possibility of a spinal fracture—as in paralysis—is distinct. Watch your children very carefully here. The only good thing about watching some young fool approach the base of the arch is that you are then able to apprehend just how huge the thing really is—even hefty football players look like miniature department-store toys at its base.

Drive now to the end of the road, and park (if you are camping, this is where the 52-site campground is located). Here you will spend the rest of the day, hiking among a bizarre and beautiful assortment of arches, fins, and free-standing pinnacles. These include Skyline Arch, Landscape Arch (at 306 feet, one of the longest arches in the world), Tunnel Arch, Broken Arch, Navajo Arch, and so forth. All are located in the Devil's Garden—a weird area of grotesquely eroded rocks. The base stone here, as elsewhere in the park, is Entrada sandstone (which dates to the Jurassic Period). Most of the formations in the Devil's Garden are upright fins, which have eroded into vertical, parallel walls. Between these you walk, often in silent awe.

Arches does not offer extensive or lengthy hiking trails in the manner, say, of Canyonlands National Park or Grand Staircase-Escalante National Monument. Most of the hikes are short day hikes from the road—the Park Avenue Trail, the trails around the Windows, the Delicate Arch Trail, and so forth. It is more a park to be seen from the road and on short 2- or 3-mile jaunts into the backcountry. About the only lengthy hike available in the park is Courthouse Wash—theoretically it could be hiked from where it crosses the road (about 2 miles north of the Park Avenue turnout) over 20 miles north to U.S. 191. There is no developed trail in the sandy wash—you just follow the drainage. On such a hike you could expect to jump a few mule deer from their day beds (the wash passes through one of their favorite habitat areas), be followed by a curious raven or two (looking for fresh carrion), and perhaps see a rattlesnake on the prowl for its best friend (the chipmunk).

Five or six million years from now, when everything west of the

San Andreas Fault has slipped into the Pacific and what remains of the Sierras resembles the Smokies, the long nourishing rains will

Courthouse Wash, Arches National Park

come at last from the west, and the place the human race called the desert will blossom. We will have played out our curious destiny by then, annihilated by some alien borg in the stars, or replaced by our own genetically engineered successors, or destroyed by our odd capacity for calculated evil. The desert, though, will remain. It will quietly undergo the beautiful changes that all things with eternal life experience. I take some comfort in that. All that we have done and created, from the crematoriums of the Holocaust to the ceiling of the Sistine Chapel, will have disappeared from this universe, but the desert will remain. Think about that the next time you drive through Arches, and perhaps mistake, as people sometimes do, the wide open spaces for emptiness.

LAND OF STANDING ROCK:

CANYONLANDS NATIONAL PARK

❖

We are now down among the buttes, and in a region the surface
of which is naked, solid rock—a beautiful red sandstone, forming a
smooth, undulating pavement. The Indians call this the Toom'pin
Tuweap', or "Rock Land," and sometimes the Toom'pin wunear'
Tuweap', or "Land of Standing Rock."

JOHN WESLEY POWELL, journal entry, July 17, 1869,
The Exploration of the Colorado River and Its Canyons (1874)

Canyonlands National Park was formed in 1964, not incidentally the same year that Congress passed the Wilderness Act. The park has all the beauty of Arches National Park to the north, but with fewer people. At 559 square miles Canyonlands is roughly five times larger than Arches. Its larger size means that Canyonlands offers many more opportunities for solitude than Arches—I have hiked for days in the park and never seen a soul (especially before spring break or after Labor Day). The park was established to protect the confluence of the Green River, which rushes down from Jim Bridger's former haunts in the Wind River Range, and the Colorado River, which is born to the east in the high snowy peaks of Rocky Mountain National Park. The two rivers meet after creating a series of deep,

Needles District, Canyonlands National Park

sheer-walled canyons in the Colorado Plateau sandstone. These canyons are called incised meanders by geologists and result from the extremely abrasive material carried by the rivers. Below their confluence is Cataract Canyon, a world-famous 14-mile stretch of whitewater that can cause even the most experienced rafter or kayaker to begin muttering a few quick prayers.

The park is divided into three districts: Island in the Sky to the north, the Needles to the southeast, and the Maze on the far west. Each is distinct, and each could provide the basis for a leisurely vacation. Taken together, they present more possibilities for adventure than one could exhaust in a lifetime.

By far, most people see the Island in the Sky district first. For one thing, it is near Moab and Interstate 70, which is where most people begin their explorations of the Colorado Plateau. For another, it offers the most commanding views of Canyonlands National Park that you can obtain without climbing into a helicopter or airplane. In fact, the panoramic views here are as spectacular as any that can be had on the South Rim or the North Rim of the Grand Canyon. To reach Island in the Sky drive north from Moab on U.S. 191 for 9

miles and then turn west on State Route 313. Proceed south at a
leisurely rate. It is a fine flat mesa, with fertile Indian rice grasslands
and open woodlands of juniper and pinyon. If it is near dawn or
dusk, you will see mule deer, so drive slowly.

Twelve miles down the road is a turnoff to the east. This side
road leads to Dead Horse Point State Park, which offers a commanding view of a broad gooseneck, or bend, in the Colorado River.
It is a great place for photographs (though best in the morning
before the sun casts a shadow over the gooseneck, which is to the
west of the point). If you stay on the main road, you'll reach the
national park boundary in another 5 miles. After paying your fee (I
always purchase an annual Golden Eagle pass), you proceed south
through Gray's Pasture (another immense sun-washed grassland)
and intermittent woodland to the end of the world—Grand View
Point Overlook.

The view here is tremendous. Due east about 30 miles are the
peaks of what the early Spanish explorers called the Sierra La Sal
Mountains. Toward the west are the Henry Mountains, rising like an
island 70 miles away. To the south are the Abajo Mountains,
about 60 miles from Grand View Point as the swallow flies. In
the middle distance, to the south and west, you can see the Maze; an
appropriately named jumble of sandstone walls, spires, and buttes.
Just this side of the Abajo Mountains is the Needles District, a tor-
tured, eroded landscape of rock pinnacles in the brightest hues of
orange and red. Directly below Grand View Point is the impressive
White Rim, a brightly colored sandstone bench at the base of the
1,000-foot cliffs.

On the rim of the Grand Canyon you peer into an abyss. It is a
vision of time more than anything else. At Grand View Point you
consider a landscape that stretches 100 miles from horizon to horizon and extends south over 60 miles—more than 6,000 square miles,
which is an area about the size of Massachusetts. It is a distance so
immense one detects the curvature of the Earth. Grandview is a revelation of space as much as the Grand Canyon is of time. At Grand

View everything you see has felt the touch of the Colorado River or one of its hard-working tributaries.

And always the wind blows, from someplace far away, with the smell of the sun and the rock and the sage on it.

As you return north on the main park road there is a turnoff to the west 6 miles north of the Grand View Point Overlook. This leads to the Green River Overlook (as nice as Dead Horse Point, but not as spectacular as Grand View) and to the Upheaval Dome, a circular pit that resembles a crater made by a nuclear detonation in the Nevada desert. It was formed by a collapsing salt dome and is more than 1,000 feet deep and 3 miles across, so it is a little more than a pit or even a hole. You could place all the term papers that I graded during my six years as an English professor inside the Upheaval Dome and still have several truckloads left over (the Department of Defense could use them to torture prisoners of war— by making them read every single garbled word).

We come now to the Needles District, which is where most of you will be spending most of your time. You enter this district via U.S. 191 55 miles south of Moab. Turn west on State Route 211 and

Needles Overlook, Canyonlands National Park

prepare to enter Shangri-La. Roughly 19 miles down the road is Newspaper Rock State Park. Be sure to stop. You walk about 30 feet and run into one of the most incredible pieces of rock art on the Plateau. Best time to take photographs is the afternoon, when the sunlight fully illuminates the panel (otherwise the rock face, which faces west, is in deep shadow and the photographs never turn out properly). Another 14 miles and you cross the portals into the Needles District—to the south you will see Sixshooter Peak, which you will remember from many a Western movie of the John Wayne period in American cinema.

The visitor's center is located just past the entrance. In the center is a three-dimensional relief map of the park, an excellent array of books and maps, and rangers always willing to assist in making hiking plans. As you drive west toward the campground (Squaw Flat is one of the nicest campgrounds in the national park system) you will begin to grasp the unique nature of the country you are about to enter. It is, no doubt, unlike anything you have seen before. The "needles" rising at all points of the horizon are composed of deeply weathered fins (upright walls of sandstone) arranged along various fault and fracture lines. Among these needle formations are numerous natural arches (Wooden Shoe is visible from the road), as well as grabens (collapsed parallel valleys). The Anasazi lived here, and their petroglyphs and cliff dwellings are quite common. There are deer everywhere, as well as ravens, rodents (from pack rats to prairie dogs), and all manner of reptiles.

The place, in short, is a hiker's paradise.

The park rangers can suggest dozens of wonderful trails, but let me recommend two of the best. The first is one they will probably tell you about—the Confluence Trail. This is the trail that leads to the confluence of the Green River and Colorado River (or at least to the overlook a hundred stories above the confluence). The trail begins at the end of the Needles road 5 miles west of the visitor's center. There is a large parking lot, an outhouse, and a well-marked trailhead. The trail proceeds west for 5 miles across Big Spring Canyon,

Confluence Overlook, Canyonlands National Park

Elephant Canyon, the Devil's Lane (a graben), and Cyclone Canyon (another graben) to the overlook, which is well worth the walk. In places it is more climbing than walking—at one point the terrain is so steep you have to climb a metal ladder over a sheer rock face. Finally you break out on a high promontory and proceed (carefully) to the overlook (no guardrails, pardner). Far below you can see the Green as it joins the Colorado. The Green River is actually green in color and the Colorado River (as its name in Spanish suggests) is red. The two rivers run side by side for awhile, as if deciding whether this marriage will work, and then ultimately join one another in the fatal embrace (for the Green) about a mile below the confluence.

Whatever you do, don't do what I did—which is start out alone at ten o'clock on a hot June morning with only one quart of water. The Confluence Trail is 10 miles round-trip over mostly sun-baked rock. About halfway back from the overlook I realized, for the first time in my hiking career, that I would not be able to complete the hike. My water was gone, it was 93 degrees in the shade, and the prickly pear cactus had begun to speak to me in intelligible sentences. I crawled, more like collapsed, underneath a pinyon pine and patiently waited for the sun to set, or for a hooded figure from Ingmar Bergman's *Seventh Seal*. Then, in the more civilized temperatures of the twilight, I wearily trudged back to the trailhead. Moral of the story: Always consult with rangers before heading into the backcountry (during much of the summer, even the rangers don't venture out in the heat of the day, unless necessary).

By the way, if you want to read an excellent essay about hiking the Confluence Trail, pick up a copy of *Abbey's Road* by Edward Abbey (see Further Reading) and turn to "A Walk in the Park." And of course, anyone viewing the confluence should read Chapter Ten in John Wesley Powell's *The Exploration of the Colorado River and Its Canyons,* which describes his rather harrowing descent of Cataract Canyon below the confluence.

The other great trail begins at the parking lot just south of the campground. This is the trail to Chesler Park, which like the Confluence Trail is about 10 miles round-trip. There are actually three different methods of reaching Chesler Park, a large grassy park in the center of the Needles District—and you should consult rangers for the best hiking conditions (some routes are wet in the spring or not recommended in the summer). By far the easiest (albeit longest) route proceeds west for about 3 miles from the parking lot on Elephant Hill Loop Road (a one-way, four-wheel-drive dirt road) to Soda Spring. At that point you turn south on the Chesler Park Trail and hike for about 3 miles. Chesler Park is an excellent location for photography—it is not as well-known as other parts of the park, and so there are more opportunities for original perspectives of the unique landscapes. Overnight backpacking trips can be made into this area, although you have to carry one gallon of water for each day as there is no water in Chesler Park.

The Maze, the third district in Canyonlands, is the most inaccessible part of the park. To be honest, I have yet to see the Maze. I am saving it for my fifties, as a reward for making it through my forties. My best friend, Jimmy Miller (we first met in Father Obermeyer's algebra class nearly thirty years ago), has been there many a time. He goes with his friend Zac, and they always backpack to a place called Spanish Bottom on the Colorado River. You need a four-wheel-drive to get into the Maze. It is about as remote a piece of country as you will find on the Colorado Plateau. To reach the area, drive south of Green River, Utah, on Hans Flat Road (unpaved) for 59 miles, from where you have another 20 or 30 miles of difficult four-wheel-drive road to negotiate before you enter the remote Maze. Some outfitters in Moab will take you there for a fee (check at park headquarters). A brave soul could rent a four-wheel-drive in Moab and drive out (although the prospect of having to write a check for an all-terrain vehicle buried in mud up to the steering wheel by a flash flood is not very appealing).

The Maze, one of the wildest and least-visited regions in the American Southwest, is described in park brochures as a "30-square-mile puzzle in sandstone." The landscape is like nothing else in North America. I've seen it many times with binoculars from Grand View Point Overlook and the Needles Overlook, and it is indeed a bizarre country. It consists of numerous very narrow sandstone walls, all cracked and fractured and deeply eroded. As a result, there are a multitude of miniature valleys—almost like hallways or corridors—between the various standing walls of rock. It looks like some abandoned desert city in the Sahara, or the decrepit ruins of Mohenjo Daro along the Indus River, or part of some fractal landscape—a scene derived from an equation that organizes chaos in strange, random patterns.

Anyone interested in visiting the Maze for a hiking or camping trip should first read Edward Abbey's fine essay "Terra Incognita: Into the Maze" in *Desert Solitaire* (see Further Reading). It will not disappoint.

There are many other exciting recreational opportunities in Canyonlands. Some people take a raft, kayak, or canoe trip down the Colorado River. (One-day to two-week trips are available; for a list of registered outfitters check with park headquarters). Others opt for an aerial tour. (These generally cost around one hundred dollars per person and, for an additional fee, can include an overflight of Monument Valley, Lake Powell, and the canyons of the Escalante). Still others sign up for a guided jeep tour of the Needles or Island in the Sky backcountry. (Lin Ottinger, a local legend of Moab, conducts his tours at such locations as the White Rim south of Grand View Point—see the Practical Information section.)

Myself? I prefer to drive into Squaw Flat Campground, pitch my tent, sit back, and watch the desert and the clouds. Every once in a while, to be sure, I will get up and take a hike of a few hours or perhaps a full day's duration (when you have to carry all your water, your hikes tend to be shorter). But my favorite memories of the Canyonlands are just sitting there, watching the desert and the clouds, lost to the world but found to myself.

It is well, sometimes, to imagine a country as it was before we were in it. To recall freedoms lost and gained, and to understand where we may be on the more extended journey, and to gaze through our longest lens, which is the past, into the future. To remember the desert as it was when Powell passed through, or Dominguez and Escalante, and to listen again to a harmony that expresses itself in silence. To consider, as the poet Yeats phrased it, "time past and passing, time to come."

THE OLD PEOPLE:

HOVENWEEP NATIONAL MONUMENT

❖

About here we crossed the boundary-line into Utah, and then,

two or three miles farther, we came upon a very interesting

group [of Anasazi ruins]. The valley, at this place, widens

out considerably, and in the center stands a solitary butte of

dark-red sandstone, upon a perfectly bare and smooth

floor of the same. . . . Running about its base,

in irregular lines, are remains of walls.

WILLIAM HENRY JACKSON, *Report of the Hayden Survey* (1875)

*S*cattered through the Four Corners region are numerous cliff dwellings. Virtually every river and major stream in the region has its accompanying cliff houses, burial places, and watch towers. In the extreme southeast corner of Utah is Hovenweep National Monument, first established in 1923. More recently it gained nation-wide fame when a Republican congressman introduced a bill to defund the monument for being too remote and lightly visited to bear continued federal support. Having visited Hovenweep, and hiked among the ruins, I couldn't disagree more. On the day I was there in mid-September the parking lot was full and the trails were filled with people, like me, who wanted to learn something more about the rich human and natural history of our country. The real

46

value of places like Hovenweep is just that—as educational tools for the masses.

Half the pleasure of Hovenweep is getting there. The monument is in a remote part of the Colorado Plateau. Drive north from Bluff, Utah, on U.S. 191 for about 15 miles until you reach the turnoff to State Route 262. Turn east and proceed onward on the winding and bumpy blacktop through a beautiful mesa country—like something out of a Georgia O'Keeffe painting. This is all part of the Navajo Reservation, so you will see eight-sided hogans, flocks of sheep, and neatly tended gardens. Fifteen miles down the road is the Hatch Trading Post, which was built by Joseph Hatch in 1903 (groceries are available here, as well as some Navajo crafts).

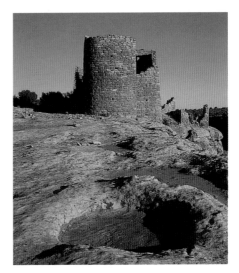

Hovenweep Castle, Hovenweep National Monument

Another 10 miles bring you to the visitor's center, perched on the edge of Hovenweep Canyon (named by William Henry Jackson for the Ute word meaning "deserted valley").

The monument is a sprawling affair, with six groups of scattered archaeological sites: the Square Tower sites and Cajon sites in Utah, and the Holly, Hackberry Canyon, Cutthroat Castle, and Goodman Point sites in Colorado. All of these sites are unique in that they have distinctive square, oval, circular, or D-shaped towers.

You will probably spend most of your time at the Square Tower site, which is within sight of the visitor's center. A 1-mile trail follows the rim of the canyon, dips down into the canyon, and then climbs back out. It will lead you past all the ruins: Hovenweep Castle (apparently used for astronomical observations—important to farmers), the check dam (conserved soil and water), Hovenweep

House (living area), Square Tower, Square Tower Spring (rare in the desert), and the remnants of a cliff dwelling, a kiva (religious structure), and a pueblo. Also in the vicinity of the visitor's center are several other trails that feature the natural history, particularly the plants, of this area.

Photographs at the head of the canyon are best taken in the late afternoon and the early evening, as the sunlight fully illuminates the ruins on the rim, while still catching the tops of those in the canyon. The scene to the east is quite dramatic, with Sleeping Ute Mountain rising from the Southern Ute Indian Reservation near Towaoc.

LIFE ON THE ROCKS:

NATURAL BRIDGES NATIONAL MONUMENT

❖

And no one came here for nearly five hundred years to break

the silence of the stones, to shadow the doorways that looked

like empty eyes out on empty canyons, to sift the midden

heaps drifted over with the silt of centuries or to peruse the

petroglyphs staring down blindly from high walls—the time of

comings and goings, all gone.

ANN ZWINGER, *Wind in the Rock: The Canyonlands of*
Southeastern Utah (1978)

Natural Bridges is one of the least visited, but most interesting, units of the national park system on the Colorado Plateau. The monument was formed in 1908 at the same time as Mesa Verde National Monument (now park)—President Theodore Roosevelt had apparently read an article in *National Geographic* about Natural Bridges in 1904 and been taken with the place. Natural Bridges is not physically large (7,636 acres), but it does offer some spectacular sandstone canyons and three of the greatest natural bridges on the planet. The canyons and bridges of Natural Bridges National Monument are cut into Cedar Mesa sandstone, which dates to about 260 million years ago. The rock is white in color and presents a pleasant visual contrast with the native pinyon and juniper. As you drive

Sipapu Bridge, Natural Bridges National Monument

along the park road, which follows the rim of the central canyon, you can see the natural bridges, as well as several cliff dwellings, scattered in the canyon below.

Kachina Natural Bridge, believed to be the youngest of the three, has a span of 206 feet. Owachomo (108 feet) is thought, because of its thinness, to be the oldest. Each bridge was carved from the sandstone by the canyon stream. Originally the natural bridges represented bends in the stream—over the ages water carved through the rock and created the open lenses now seen. Natural bridges are different from arches in that arches are formed by exfoliation (see

Arches National Park) and natural bridges are formed by water erosion. Although Sipapu (220 feet), Owachomo, and Kachina are free-standing and intact, far up White Canyon are the ruins of another bridge that fell to Earth at some point in the distant past.

My favorite of the three great bridges is Owachomo. As with the other natural bridges, the secret to obtaining a good photograph is to hike down the .5-mile trail from the parking turnout. Once at the base of Owachomo, keep walking under the rock span and across the slickrock to the little pool of rainwater that gathers at the base of the far cliffs. This is about 100 yards downstream from Owachomo. There are a number of superb vantages at this pool location (best shot at midday with the sun at your back and with a polarizing filter). My preferred approach is to set the tripod up at the far end of the pool and shoot upward with the water in the foreground. If it is summer, you will also have some nice green color from the cattails and reeds.

There is a primitive 13-site campground in the monument, as well as a number of nice hiking trails. One of the most popular hiking trails runs from Sipapu Natural Bridge 8.2 miles to Owachomo Natural Bridge through the bottom of White Canyon. Along the way you will see several Anasazi cliff dwellings and will often be shaded in the summer by the willows and immense cottonwoods (which turn bright yellow in the autumn). Shorter hikes of 5.6 and 4 miles, respectively, can be made between Sipapu Natural Bridge and Kachina Natural Bridge, and Kachina Natural Bridge and Owachomo Natural Bridge. All three natural bridges are accessible from short .5-mile trails from the paved monument road.

Natural Bridges is at a fairly high elevation—from 5,500 to 6,500 feet—so you can expect snow through April and beginning some years as early as October. It is the perfect place to visit on a hot summer day when people are frying eggs on the rocks of Monument Valley and hikers are keeling over right and left in the depths of the Grand Canyon from heat exhaustion. The names of the natural bridges, by the way, come from Hopi. Owachomo means "rock mound," a reference to a nearby hill. Sipapu refers to the gateway to the spirit world through which souls enter and exit. Kachina is named for the Kachina dancers so important to the Hopi religion (and on which the famous Hopi Kachina dolls are based).

There are a number of other superb hiking opportunities in the area: Fish and Owl Creeks, Grand Gulch Primitive Area, and the Dark Canyon Wilderness and Primitive Area are administered by the Bureau of Land Management (see Practical Information). At this BLM office you can find topographic maps and detailed hiking guides for these unique resources. My favorite is Grand Gulch— a nearly half-million-square-acre archaeological preserve just to the south of Natural Bridges. For many hundreds of years the Anasazi flourished in the Grand Gulch, a tributary of the San Juan River, and evidence of their culture is abundant. To reach Grand Gulch turn south from State Route 95 onto State Route 261 about 2 miles east of the entrance to Natural Bridges National Monument. Follow 261 south for 5 miles to the Kane Gulch BLM Ranger Station. Personnel in the trailer have maps, hiking guides, brochures, and good advice.

The most popular day hike runs 4 miles west through Kane Gulch to the junction with Grand Gulch. At this junction there are a kiva and its surrounding cliff dwellings—please do not disturb the contents. The trail from Kane Gulch to the San Juan River and back is 103 miles round-trip, all through roadless wilderness—one of the finest backcountry trails in America!

Dark Canyon is an extensive canyon west of Blanding, Utah, and east of Hite on Lake Powell. The higher portion of the canyon in Manti-La Sal National Forest is managed as a wilderness area (about 45,000 acres). The lower part of the canyon, on BLM land, is managed as a primitive area (about 62,000 acres). Dark Canyon drains from the uplands of the Abajo Mountains to the lower Colorado River, so you will find everything here from quaking aspen and Douglas fir to prickly pear cactus and yucca. There are a number of great extended hikes in Dark Canyon, from both the Hite area (Sundance Trail provides access) and Blanding area (Woodenshoe Canyon provides access). If interested in these trails, I recommend contacting the BLM office in Monticello [(801) 587-2141; Post Office Box 7, Monticello, Utah 84535]. The Canyonlands Natural History Association publishes the very informative *Dark Canyon Trail Guide,* available at the BLM office and in nearby national parks.

Two other sites in the area around Natural Bridges National Monument, both managed by the state, bear mentioning. First is Muley Point, which is 30 miles south on State Route 261 from its junction with State Route 95 (the road to Natural Bridges). Muley Point presents a commanding view of the San Juan River Canyon, with the Chuska Mountains to the east, Monument Valley to the south, and Navajo Mountain toward the west. This is a sublime place to watch the sunrise, or sunset, if you're in the area. Another excellent spot is Goosenecks State Park, which is 8 miles south of State Route 261 from Muley Point (via some incredible white-knuckle switchbacks—not recommended at all for RVs). Goosenecks presents a stunning view of several canyon goosenecks (elongated cutbacks of the meandering river) along the San Juan River. The Valley of the Gods (a smaller version of Monument Valley) is just a couple of miles north of Muley Point. I highly recommend both of these canyon viewpoints to anyone visiting Natural Bridges National Monument—they will truly complete your trip.

WATERWORLD: GLEN CANYON
NATIONAL RECREATION AREA

❖

The features of this canyon are greatly diversified. Still vertical

walls at times. These are usually found to stand above great curves.

The river, sweeping around these bends undermines the cliffs in

places. Sometimes the rocks are overhanging; in other curves,

curious, narrow glens are found. . . . Other wonderful features are

the many side canyons or gorges that we pass. . . . Usually,

in going up such a gorge, we find beautiful vegetation. . . . On

the walls, and back many miles into the country, numbers of

monument-shaped buttes are observed. So we have a curious

ensemble of wonderful features—carved walls, royal arches, glens,

alcove gulches, mounds and monuments. From which of these

features shall we select a name? We decide to call it Glen Canyon.

JOHN WESLEY POWELL, journal entry, August 3, 1869,
The Exploration of the Colorado River and Its Canyons (1874)

Lake Powell, formed by Glen Canyon Dam, is the second largest reservoir in the world and the second most popular destination on the Colorado Plateau (Grand Canyon is the first). The shoreline of Lake Powell stretches 1,960 miles—more than the shorelines of California, Oregon, and Washington combined. The reservoir receives over 3 million visitors each year—more than Yellowstone National Park. Most visitors come for the boating (houseboating especially), the water skiing, and the fishing. The reservoir is a great

Glen Canyon National Recreation Area near Hite Marina

place to cool off in the middle of summer. There is also plenty of country to explore on foot—only 13 percent of the 1-million-acre area is under water. The rest consists of canyons, sandstone formations, and open desert. Herein people can find Anasazi ruins, exotic fauna and flora (in and around spring seeps, hanging gardens, and potholes), and dinosaur fossil sites (tracks of eight dinosaur species have been identified at Glen Canyon).

Although there is a large non-reservoir segment of Glen Canyon National Recreation Area that extends north to Hans Flat (see Canyonlands National Park), most recreational activities are centered around the reservoir. In the north, marina access to the reservoir is found at Hite, which is accessed by State Route 95 west of Blanding, Utah. Hite is located just below the confluence of the Dirty Devil and Colorado Rivers. The country looks like what you would expect to find at the headwaters of the Nile River in Egypt—rocks, rocks, and more rocks. You will find a ranger station, campgrounds, beaches, and several marinas offering powerboat and houseboat rentals. These boats can be taken deep into the reservoir—all the way to Rainbow Bridge (largest natural bridge in the world) if you wish. In the spring and fall, fishing is good for bass, crappie, pike, walleye, and channel catfish. Boats can also be used to access remote areas for hiking or backpacking trips.

If you continue on State Route 95 over the Dirty Devil River you will reach the turnoff for State Route 276 after about 20 miles. Turn west on 276 and follow it south to Bullfrog Marina to find the second major put-in point for the northern part of the reservoir (with all the same services available at Hite). A ferry here will take you a couple of miles across the reservoir to Hall's Crossing (a shortcut back to State Route 95). From either of these two points it is possible to explore by boat the various slickrock canyons in the center of the reservoir, including beautiful Escalante Canyon (named for Father Escalante, who passed through these parts in 1776).

The final set of marinas is found in and around Page, Arizona, which is accessed by U.S. 89. These are concentrated around Wahweap in the country just to the west of the Glen Canyon Campground and include a ranger station and all the other visitor services you would expect, including camping and an RV park. Interesting note on Wahweap—it is near one of the few known camping sites of the 1776 Dominguez-Escalante expedition. The nearby "Crossing of the Fathers"—now under water—is named for the location where the expedition crossed the river.

Anyone staying in Page should check out the numerous aerial tours over Glen Canyon and the Grand Canyon, as well as the photographic tours to the nearby Navajo Reservation. Antelope Canyon, which requires a licensed guide and a permit from the Navajo Nation, is one of the most spectacular slot canyons in the West. Such a trip is worth every penny—you can find literature on these tours at the brochure stands in every motel or hotel lobby.

If you want to learn about Glen Canyon before it was dammed, read John Wesley Powell's narrative or Edward Abbey's essay "Down the River" in *Desert Solitaire* (see Further Reading), which relates one of the last float trips down Glen Canyon before the dam. Abbey wrote a great essay entitled "The Damnation of a Canyon" in *Beyond the Wall,* which describes the season he worked in Glen Canyon as a park ranger:

> *There was a time when, in my search for essences, I concluded that the canyonland country has no heart. I was wrong. The canyonlands did have a heart, a living heart, and that heart was Glen Canyon and the golden, flowing Colorado River. In the summer of 1959 I made a float trip in a little rubber raft down through the length of Glen Canyon, starting at Hite and getting off the river near Gunsight Butte—The Crossing of the Fathers. In this voyage of some 150 miles and ten days our only mode of power, and all that we needed, was the current of the Colorado River.*

Abbey compares the canyon before and after and concludes that, once the dam has reached the end of its natural life span, things won't be so bad: "Within a generation—thirty years—I predict the river and canyons will bear a decent resemblance to their former selves."

Two final books will be of great interest to Lake Powell aficionados: Eliot Porter's *The Place No One Knew: Glen Canyon on the Colorado* (1963), which includes some of the last photographs taken of the inner canyon before the dam was completed, and Eleanor Inkslip's *The Colorado River Through Glen Canyon Before Lake Powell: Historic Photo Journal, 1872 to 1964* (see Further Reading).

Enjoy!

BEING THERE: RAINBOW BRIDGE

NATIONAL MONUMENT

❖

I imagined there was no scene in all the world to
equal this. . . . The meaning of the ages was flung at me.
A man became nothing.

ZANE GREY, *Navajo Wildlands* (1917)

*R*ainbow Bridge, long held sacred by Native Americans, was not
seen by a Euroamerican—Dr. Byron Cummings—until 1907. It
was, at that time, a 6-mile hike up from the Colorado River. When
Zane Grey came up for a look, he was so impressed that he carved his
name in the rock under the bridge—still visible to this day. Theodore
Roosevelt stopped by and called it the greatest wonder in the world.
In 1910 the bridge was set aside as a national monument. The 160
acres of the monument now preserve one of the most fantastic struc-
tures on the Colorado Plateau. Since Lake Powell filled up, Rainbow
Bridge is now only a quarter-mile stroll from the floating docks.
Overland horseback rides are also available from Navajo Mountain
Trading Post in Tonalea, Arizona.

Rainbow Bridge is carved from salmon-pink Navajo sandstone. It measures 287 feet across the bridge and hangs 309 feet over the bottom of the gorge. It is the shape of an enormous lens, with views deeper into the rock canyon behind it. Even before the arrival of Euroamericans, the Navajo and Paiute referred to the span, in their respective languages, as the Rainbow Bridge, so strongly does it evoke a rainbow. The best time to visit is in the spring, when the prickly pear cactus are flowering and the canyon wrens are singing. It is a mystic, sacred place, and, at that season, Rainbow Bridge, indeed, seems a bridge to another world—a place inside us, a place all around us, a place forever just beyond us.

The easiest way to visit Rainbow Bridge National Monument is to take a half-day or full-day boat tour across Lake Powell from the public marinas at Wahweap, Bullfrog, or Hall's Crossing, each about 50 miles from the bridge by water.

IF YOU BUILD IT, THEY WILL COME:

GRAND STAIRCASE-ESCALANTE

NATIONAL MONUMENT

❖

At four thousand feet the blue is certainly more positive,

more intense, than at sea-level; at six thousand feet it begins to

darken and deepen, and it seems to fit in the saddles and notches

of the mountains like a block of lapis lazuli; at eight thousand

feet it has darkened still more and has a violet hue about it.

The night sky at this altitude is almost weird in its purples.

A deep violet fits up close to the rim of the moon, and the orb itself

looks like a silver wafer pasted upon the sky.

JOHN VAN DYKE, The Desert (1901)

On September 18, 1996, President Bill Clinton stood on the North Rim of the Grand Canyon and signed the executive order creating the new Grand Staircase-Escalante National Monument in southern Utah. This immense 1.7-million-acre area, now administered by the National Park Service, is the core of the *largest* combined national park land in the Lower 48 states (the monument is contiguous with Capitol Reef National Park, Bryce Canyon National Park, Glen Canyon National Recreation Area, and Canyonlands National Park, for a total area of nearly 5 million acres).

The monument's vast and austere landscapes embrace a spectacular array of scientific and historic resources. Geologically, the area is a treasure house of clearly exposed stratigraphy and sedimentary base structures. A wide variety of formations, often in brilliant colors, have been exposed by millennia of erosion. The monument includes the rugged canyon country of the upper Paria Canyon system, the Grand Staircase identified over a century ago by pioneering geologist Clarence Dutton, major components of the White and Vermillion Cliffs and associated benches, the incredibly beautiful Escalante canyonlands, and the vast Kaiparowits Plateau, which encompasses about 1,600 square miles of sedimentary rock, ascending plateaus and benches, and steep-walled serpentine canyons.

There are many arches and natural bridges scattered throughout the monument, including the 130-foot-high Escalante Natural Bridge, with a 100-foot span, and Grosvenor Arch, a rare "double arch." The monument also includes rich paleontological sites, extensive regions of petrified wood, and an impressive array of prehistoric sites, including cliff dwellings, kivas, rock art panels, campsites, kill sites, and granaries. Five life zones are found in Grand Staircase-Escalante National Monument, from low desert to Canadian forest. The monument features pristine grasslands, virgin pinyon-juniper woodlands dated at 1,400 years, canyon bottom refugia and hanging garden microsites, and such exotic wildlife as desert bighorn sheep, migratory neotropical birds, and the rare desert tortoise.

Grand Staircase-Escalante National Monument preserves the heart of the redrock desert north of the Grand Canyon, and its establishment will relieve much of the recreational pressure that has been building in recent years on the other two major redrock parks: Arches and Canyonlands. The new monument offers superb mountain-biking trails, in the form of old BLM dirt roads, and some of the best hiking and backpacking on the Colorado Plateau. There are basically three outdoor seasons in the monument. In the spring we have the world-famous wildflowers displays. Summer is an ideal time for exploring the swimming holes and cool wet gorges. Fall, with the lowest waters of the season, permits hikers to penetrate to the lower Escalante canyons, where they can examine Anasazi rock art and cliff dwellings.

The major challenge for most people interested in exploring the new monument is access—there are no paved roads into the area (which is also a blessing). Various local outfitters offer four-wheel-drive and horseback trips into the monument. One of the best is Escalante Canyon Outfitters in Boulder, Utah (see Practical Information). This backcountry operation is run by a husband and wife—Grant Johnson and Sue Fearon—who have lived in the area for decades and been active in the Southern Utah Wilderness Alliance that lobbied so tirelessly, with state environmental leaders like Robert Redford and Terry Tempest Williams, to bring the new monument into being. Both are accomplished naturalists and are well versed in the fascinating geology, archaeology, and ecology of the area. Most of their trips are concentrated in the Canyons of the Escalante part of the monument, which ranges on the west from Hole in the Rock Road, which runs south for 50 miles from Escalante to the vicinity of Lake Powell, to Burr Trail Road on the east, which leads from Boulder toward Capitol Reef National Park. Grant and Sue use horses to pack in the food and supplies necessary to make a comfortable base camp. They recently became proud parents of a new baby daughter, who now accompanies them on their wilderness journeys.

Other hikes in this area are accessible to people without a four-wheel-drive or the resources for an outfitted trip. These include the .5-mile trail to Lower Calf Creek Falls (the well-marked trailhead is 16 miles east of Escalante on State Route 12), a spectacular 126-foot waterfall over exposed slickrock, and the 2-mile trail to Escalante Natural Bridge (the well-marked trailhead is 15 miles east of Escalante where State Route 12 crosses the river). On the other side of State Route 12—opposite the trailhead to Escalante Natural Bridge—is the trail to Phipps Arch; simply follow the river 1.5 miles south to the mouth of Phipps Wash, which enters from the west, then access the arch by hiking up the drainage.

Another popular hike, and one well described by Edward Abbey in his coffee-table book *Slickrock* (see Further Reading), leads into

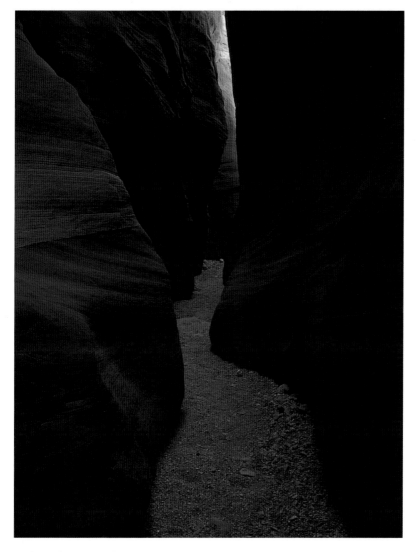

Slot Canyon, Grand Staircase-Escalante National Monument

the lower Escalante canyons to a place called Skyline or Stevens Arch (both names can be found on maps and in the literature). If you are interested in this hike, be certain to receive specific directions from the rangers at the Escalante BLM Office at 755 West Main in Escalante [currently serving as the monument visitor's center and administrative headquarters; (801) 826-5499]. The trail begins about 40 miles south of Escalante at a place called Coyote Wash on Hole in

the Rock Road, which may be impassable during periods of rain or
snowfall). The Skyline Arch Trail is 12 miles one-way to the east and
follows Coyote Gulch to the Lower Escalante River. The arch is in
the vicinity of the river—again, ask for specific directions from
rangers and be certain to carry 7 1/2-minute USGS maps). Also in the
general neighborhood of Coyote Wash are the trails to Peek-a-boo,
Spooky Gulch, and Willow Gulch, which leads to Broken Bow Arch.
Many of these trails are dangerous, or impossible, in times of high
water and at other times may involve deep wades while holding your
backpack over your head or swimming with it on an inflatable raft.
During the hottest summer months, extreme caution should be used
because of the danger of flash floods and you should always carry
adequate water of about 1 gallon per day.

Far to the south, along U.S. 89 between Big Water City and
Kanab in Arizona, another portion of the monument preserves the
Upper Paria River canyon system. Herein you may find one of
the nicest and most accessible slot canyons in the Southwest—
Buckskin Gulch. If interested in hiking the canyon, visit the BLM
ranger station 10 miles west of Big Water City. The friendly rangers
sell USGS maps, books, and a helpful BLM guide (*Hiker's Guide to
Paria Canyon*). The Paria River runs just south of the BLM office and
the canyon can be accessed there. I once hiked part of this section in
late March and it was delightful: I was up to my knees in cool water
for 8 miles round-trip). However, I would most recommend that you
drive about 4 miles west of the BLM ranger station to Wire Pass, turn
south there on the dirt road (called Rock Valley Road), and follow it
about 2 miles to the well-marked trailhead (signs, parking lot full
of cars, people putting on suntan lotion and filling daypacks with
goodies, outhouse).

Hike east with the others into the drainage. After about a mile
the slot canyon begins—in places it is 500 feet deep and only as wide
as your shoulders. High above are logs jammed between the canyon walls during periods of high water—never hike here during the
summer thunderstorm period. On the south canyon wall at the con-

Eroded river caves, Grand Staircase-
Escalante National Monument

fluence of this side canyon with Buckskin Gulch is some Anasazi
rock art (bighorn sheep). For a really great adventure leave one car
parked at Lee's Ferry, drive the other to Buckskin, and hike all the
way up Paria Canyon (35 miles one-way) to the Lee's Ferry National
Park Ranger Station on the Colorado River in Glen Canyon National Recreation Area. Someday I aim to do just that—let me know
through the publisher if you are interested in going along (leave one
car parked at Lee's Ferry, drive the other to Buckskin)—but only
those who, when things get tough, only complain in the form of
jokes need apply.

There is some pretty amazing human history in the vicinity of
Paria Canyon. First is the abundant evidence of the Anasazi period—the petroglyphs carved or pecked into the canyon walls
at regular intervals. Next we have Dominguez and Escalante, who
camped for several days near Lee's Ferry and then traveled through
the canyon to what is today called Dominguez Pass. Lee's Ferry was
established in 1871 by John Lee, who operated the first ferry over the
river. Powell passed through in that period and noted that a small
settlement called "Pahreah," consisting of 47 families, had taken up

residence along the Paria River. Severe flooding eventually forced the community to disband. Later a Western movie set was built on the site of the ghost town, and several old-time movies were filmed here (based on Zane Grey novels, including such forgotten masterpieces as *Heritage of the Desert* and *Revelation*).

More recently, the area became the haunt of landscape photographers, nature writers, and other lovers of the wilderness. Edward Abbey wrote an excellent essay about a hike he took down Buckskin Gulch in *Beyond the Wall* ("Days and Nights on the Old Pariah"). Finally, the U.S. Fish and Wildlife Service released California condors in the Paria Canyon-Vermillion Cliffs area in 1996. If you see a magnificent dark bird with a nine-foot wingspan soaring overhead—something that makes a turkey vulture look about the size of a pigeon—it is likely to be a condor.

The April 14, 1997, issue of *High Country News* was devoted to the changes the new national monument is expected to bring to southern Utah [if you don't subscribe, you should: (800) 905-1155]. Some of the local population were quite upset with the designation because it forever prevented the abundant coal resources of the Kaiparowits Plateau from being developed. Kane County, the area most heavily affected, is 95 percent public land and home to 10,000 people, most of whom are Mormon, with an average family income of $18,000. In a way, the monument may be the best long-term development possible for the locals. As the article reports, "Southern Utah's mining, logging and ranching are in decline." The future for the Colorado Plateau is in eco-tourism and in promoting the area as an international resource. During a recent hike in Buckskin Gulch I had the opportunity to practice my high-school German, my college French, and what little Japanese I picked up from my second wife. Only my graduate school Anglo-Saxon was left on the shelf. If you build it, they will come.

HEART OF THE COUNTRY:

ZION NATIONAL PARK

❖

The walls have smooth, plain faces and are everywhere

very regular and vertical for a thousand feet or more, where they

seem to break back in shelving slopes to higher altitudes; and

everywhere, as we go along, we find springs bursting out at the foot

of the walls. . . . On the western wall of the canyon stand some

buttes, towers and high pinnacled rocks. . . . These tower rocks are

known [by the Mormons] as the Temples of the Virgen [sic].

JOHN WESLEY POWELL, journal entry, September 12, 1872,
The Exploration of the Colorado River and Its Canyons (1874)

Let us just say that for some reason—a job, a family, a familiar routine—you have spent the entire winter, or perhaps several, in a far northern city. A place like Caribou, Maine, or Moose Jaw, Saskatchewan, or, that outpost I know so well, Fairbanks, Alaska. These are all fine places during the fishing season, but they lose much of their allure once the rivers freeze. You have risen every morning for six months to concrete gray clouds and arctic cold, and over that time you have watched one too many games on the sports channel. Now it is late March. Despite the fact that the vernal equinox has come and gone, snow has drifted over the driveway for the third time this week. Today at work the resident troublemakers earned their right to the national title, again. When you returned home your latest experiment in romance had left a note on the refrigerator, indicating she was returning to her ex-husband, for the second or third time.

You look at the calendar and notice it is spring. Perhaps because you are a teacher you have the week off. Or perhaps you pursue some other line of work and have accumulated a week's leave time. In any event, you suddenly—and this is the first real favor you've done for yourself in awhile—pack the essential camping gear, drive to the airport, and catch a series of flights to Las Vegas. You arrive in the middle of the night, pick up a rental car, return it ten minutes later with an unspecified transmission problem, obtain a free upgrade, and then drive east, with no one else on the road but newspaper delivery trucks and escort service limousines.

Slickrock, Zion National Park

For several hours you motor across the desert, eventually crossing the Utah state line and turning north toward St. George. At the Hurricane exit you leave the interstate and follow Route 9 into the mountains, past the little villages of Virgin, Grafton, and Rockville. Even though it is raining you drive with the window down. The scent—of sagebrush, ponderosa sap, and fallen cottonwood leaves—is powerful, overwhelming, intox-icating, and you wonder why anyone, least of all yourself, would live in any other place. After awhile you see black space and stars among the clouds—closer to the park now—and somewhere on a peak to the south you can be sure the astronomers are focusing some giant lens on a beautiful mystery.

The road climbs, winding close to the river, great sheets of rock nearby, and soon passes into the park. You pay your fee, drive on, and, just as the sun breaks over the eastern rock, spot the place you have come so far to see—Zion Canyon. You are certain of one thing— that some people have secret meetings and surprise memos and others have places like the desert. Quite suddenly that other world, the impoverished one you wisely left behind for now, has ceased to exist, and you have discovered the freedom without which there can be, properly speaking, no life.

Even though you are far from what the world calls your home— an address, a phone number, a pile of useless junk called property— you realize that you are at last home. Definition of home? The place where you feel secure, and loved, and happy.

That is Zion National Park—scarlet walls stretching beyond belief, sheer slabs of weathered rock, cascading waterfalls, a clear river running over cobblestone, giant ponderosas and cottonwoods, a quiet and protected inner valley.

By far, most of you two million annual visitors will be spending most of your time in the environs of Zion Canyon. You should also know that to the north, accessed by exit 40 on Interstate 15, there is another popular unit of the park called Kolob Canyons—more on that later.

Zion Canyon is the aesthetic heart of the national park—an enormous outdoor cathedral made of rock. It is one of those places that takes your heart by storm. Just as a woman is lovely at any sea- son of her life, so is Zion Canyon beautiful at any time of the year. Spring brings the blossoming flowers, a rich wild garden including those found in the Rocky Mountains and those of the lower deserts: prickly pear cactus and blue columbine, yucca, and Indian paint- brush. Summer is a long and mellow season, without the scorching heat of the Mojave that begins—with the first Joshua trees—just down the road in St. George. In autumn the cottonwoods turn a luminous shade of yellow and contrast brightly with the deep blue Utah sky. In winter the snow drapes everything in white, a scene that evokes the stark majesty of that other great canyon valley—Yosemite.

Virgin River Canyon, Zion National Park

Like Canyonlands, Zion is a fantastic hiking park, and much of it is centered around Zion Canyon. Among the easy trails, you will find the trail to the Court of the Patriarchs (easiest trail in the national park system—50 yards and all concrete) about 2.2 miles north on Zion Canyon Scenic Drive from the park visitor's center. The trailhead to the Lower and Emerald Pools begins .5 mile farther up the road—the trail to the Lower Pool can be walked in a few minutes; the trail to the upper pool requires about an hour and a half (this longer trail will give you a good view of the pinyon-juniper-oak habitat that predominates on drier slopes, as well as the fir and aspen of higher elevations). By far, the park's most popular trail follows the Virgin River as it enters "The Narrows"—access is from the parking lot at the end of Zion Canyon Scenic Drive. When I hiked this stretch in June of 1995, the wildflowers were incredible—numerous hanging gardens of golden columbine, bracken ferns, green moss, and red monkeyflower on the wet canyon walls and brightly colored butterflies everywhere.

There are many other, much longer trails in Zion. For example, in the desert southwest corner of the park there is the Chinle Trail, which begins a mile east of Rockville on State Route 9. It leads north through Huber Wash and Scoggins Wash to a spring on Coalpits Wash. The trail is 6.8 miles one-way and throughout the entire route you will be able to view not only great vistas to the south but also sizeable chunks of petrified wood scattered here and there. One of the longest trails in the park is the West Rim Trail, which begins just across the river from Zion Lodge in Zion Canyon, and leads over 14 miles through some rugged country to the north, eventually ending at Lava Point (a fire lookout accessed by Kolob Terrace Road, which begins in Virgin on State Route 9). This trail will take you over Horse Pasture Plateau, where a wildfire burned pretty ferociously in 1980—the views of the surrounding valleys and exposed rock are incredible.

The Kolob Canyon Visitor Center, mentioned earlier, provides access to the spectacular canyons at the edge of Kolob Terrace. The park road leads 5 miles into the red rock country, ending on a high viewpoint. Everywhere there are steep sheer-walled cliffs of white and red sandstone. Good hiking trails lead from Kolob Canyons Road up the Middle Fork of Taylor Creek to Double Arch Alcove (2.7 miles one-way) and from Lee Pass on Kolob Canyons Road to Kolob Arch on Verkin Creek (7.2 miles one-way).

Long after you leave Zion National Park, you will remember its central feature—the Great White Throne—which rises 2,500 feet from the floor of Zion Canyon. Composed of Navajo sandstone, the Throne is actually light buckskin in color, but when the sun strikes the rock, it shines a brilliant white. It appears variously—depending on the time of day and your mood—like the throne of a god, a fitting tablet on which a god might carve instructions, the tombstone of a god. It is pure inspiration, larger than any building on earth, and, not surprisingly, served as the basis for one of Ansel Adams's finest photographs. Perhaps it will serve as the basis of one of yours!

ILLUMINATED LANDSCAPE:

BRYCE CANYON NATIONAL PARK

❖

. . . a beautiful desolation.

ANSEL ADAMS (1941)

Like Cedar Breaks National Monument, Bryce Canyon National Park protects a high-altitude area covered with snow for much of the year. From early spring through early autumn, however, Bryce Canyon is packed with people (1.5 million annually) from all over the planet—whole busloads are brought in every day from Las Vegas. However, take heart—90 percent of Bryce Canyon National Park visitors remain on the rim, staring, pointing, and taking snapshots. If you hike down into the hoodoos (the pinnacles of eroded sandstone that everyone comes to see) you will quickly escape much of the congestion.

It is important to do just that. Unlike the Grand Canyon, in which you face a half- or full-mile hike into the earth, many of the hiking trails in Bryce Canyon only descend a few hundred feet—just enough so that you can fully appreciate the unusual beauty and impressive stature of the rock formations.

And beautiful they are, these weird spires, bizarre pinnacles, and strangely fluted castellations, all in the brightest colors imaginable—red, pink, mauve, buff, white, orange, and yellow, set among forests of green and skies so blue. These are rocks that have to be seen to be believed. Bryce is, without question, the most colorful park on the planet.

The park is about 50 miles north of Zion but might as well be on a different planet, so different is the scenery. What we have in Zion are deeply eroded canyons. What we have in Bryce is a 20-mile escarpment of very soft rock that has been shaped into fantastic forms by the elements. Along the escarpment there are over a dozen amphitheaters filled with the eroded pink and white limestone of the Paunsaugunt Plateau. You reach the park via U.S. 89, turning east on State Route 12 and following it for 16 miles before turning south on State Route 63.

The first turnoff is .5 mile south of the park entrance—Fairyland

Thor's Hammer, Bryce Canyon National Park

Point. Inside the vast bowl below are hundreds of turreted vertical columns that stand in serried ranks as if figures in some artist's workshop, waiting to be finished. Down lower, rainwaters have scoured out v-shaped gorges. Sharp ridges have been cut into side ridges and then the side ridges have been further dissected into bizarre shapes of intricate complexity. No need to visit Badlands National Monument in South Dakota—at Fairyland Point you've seen it, in full technicolor.

Almost every weathering process known to geology is partly responsible for these strange, bizarre badlands: fragmentation from freezing and thawing, wind and rain erosion, exfoliation (the peeling of slabs or sheets of rock), oxidation of minerals in the rocks, hydration (a form of chemical weathering), carbonation (another chemical weathering process), organic weathering (roots and rodents), and solution weathering (the dissolving of softer rocks). The geologists tell us the last is one of the most important processes and helps to create the distinctive symmetrical patterns visible in pillar after pillar.

Farther down the road are many other great views: Sunrise Point, Sunset Point, Inspiration Point, Bryce Point, Farview Point, Rainbow Point, and Yovimpa Point. My favorite—and I've tried them all—is Bryce Point, which offers a commanding view of the Bryce Creek headwaters. All these streams, by the way, wind up eventually in the Paria River (see the discussion of Buckskin Gulch in the Grand Staircase-Escalante National Monument section).

There are over 50 miles of trails in Bryce Canyon National Park. If you only have a few hours, I strongly suggest the 1.5-mile Navajo Loop Trail, which begins and ends at Sunset Point just south of the lodge. This trail will lead you past Thor's Hammer—one of the most striking hoodoos (pillars) in the park. The trail penetrates to the center of what is called Wall Street (very steep-sided walls on either side of the trail). At several places in the Wall Street section of the trail there are large Douglas firs that grow straight up between the walls. For a striking photograph, set up your tripod about 12 feet from the base of a tree. Aim the lens toward the top of the tree so that the body of the camera is parallel, or nearly so, to the plane of the ground. (Be sure to use a polarizing filter.) Focus about one-third up the tree and set your aperture at F/22. Be sure to meter off the tree trunk and to bracket: Take a number of exposures at slightly different settings. I think you'll be pleased with the result (I recommend Kodachrome 25). This cannot be done effectively without a tripod, because at F/22, even on a bright day, you'll be shooting at 1/8 second or so with a polarizing filter. Also, this is a photograph best taken in the middle of the day, when the canyon walls all around the tree are receiving direct sunlight and have some color in them.

Those with more time can choose from a number of good hiking trails. Two of the best are the Under the Rim Trail, which runs from Fairyland Point south all the way to Rainbow Point (over 20 miles by trail). Remember that overnight use in the park requires a permit available at the visitor's center. Another fine trail is the Riggs Spring Loop Trail, which begins and ends at Rainbow Point (end of the road). This 8-mile trail leads around the Promontory, through Corral Hollow and Mutton Hollow, past Riggs Spring, and over Yovimpa Pass on the Pink Cliffs. It makes a splendid all-day hike. There is also a nice backcountry camping site, including a group camping site, at Riggs Spring.

As you make your plans for Bryce Canyon, remember that its high elevation makes it more prone to colder weather than some of the other parks in the region. When I visited the park the first time— in early June—it snowed so heavily I finally had to leave and head for warmer climes at the Grand Canyon. Also remember that if you have small children you should always keep them close by your side as you hike around the rims and on the trails. This, of course, would apply to all the parks and monuments in this book.

There may be a more beautiful national park somewhere in the world, but I doubt it!

A WILDERNESS OF ROCKS:

CAPITOL REEF NATIONAL PARK

❖

[It is] a maze of cliffs and terraces, red and white domes,
rock platforms gashed with profound canyons, burning plains bar-
ren even of sagebrush—all glowing with bright color and flooded
with blazing sunlight.

CLARENCE DUTTON, *Report on the Geology of the*
High Plateaus of Utah (1880)

*T*arantula Mesa. Bitter Creek Divide. Sulphur Creek. Gypsum
Sinkhole. South Desert. Wildcat Mesa. Bloody Hands Gap. The
Castle. Temple of the Sun. The place names evoke the austere landscape of the Waterpocket Fold Country—a harsh dry land of stark
beauty and often solemn grandeur.

The park acquires its name from two geological formations: the
Waterpocket Fold, a 100-mile uplift that juts out over the surrounding desert and resembles a gigantic multicolored coral reef, and
Capitol Dome, an enormous white sandstone dome that resembles
the dome on the U.S. Capitol building. Long and skinny—that best
describes the physical configuration of Capitol Reef National Park,
which is at no point wider than 12 miles but which follows the 100-

Panorama Viewpoint, Capitol Reef National Park

mile Waterpocket Fold from Cathedral Valley nearly to the shores of Lake Powell.

The Fremont River cuts through the northern part of the park, and it was here that early Mormon settlers gathered. The remnants of their tiny community, called Fruita, can still be seen in the canyon near the visitor's center on State Route 24: a barn, a farmhouse, rock fences, a one-room schoolhouse dating to 1896, and many acres of fruit orchards. Mule deer can be seen in the orchards at any time of the day—drive carefully through this area. It is a beautiful site—the very picture of the peaceful pastoral life. There is a nice campground here (71 sites) among the cottonwood trees on the banks of the Fremont River.

Some of the nicest hiking trails in Capitol Reef National Park are found in the vicinity of the visitor's center. One of the most popular is the Navajo Knobs Trail (4.5 miles one-way), which begins just north of the visitor's center and climbs the nearby hills for a panoramic view of the region. Grand Wash Trail (2.25 miles one-way) is much easier, with mostly flat walking on a dry wash between the canyon walls. The well-marked trailhead is about 3.5 miles east of the visitor's center on State Route 24. Another good short hike leads from Panorama Point (about 2 miles west of the visitor's center on State Route 24) to the Goosenecks Overlook and Sunset Point—great views are to be found here (though be careful on the rocks—it is a long way down).

South of the visitor's center is paved Scenic Drive, which I strongly recommend. This will take you into the heart of the Water-pocket Fold country and enable you to see such sights as the Egyptian Temple and the Golden Throne. Beyond Scenic Drive are an unpaved road that leads to Pleasant Creek and an unpaved fork that leads up Capitol Gorge.

Those with four-wheel-drive vehicles can take the primitive dirt road to Cathedral Valley, where some amazing sandstone monoliths jut from the floor of the desert—a photographer's paradise, especially at sunrise and sunset, with a primitive campground near the monoliths. The Temple of the Sun is a truly awesome formation—as striking in its own way as El Capitan or Half Dome in Yosemite Valley. Ansel Adams took a series of very fine photographs in Cathedral Valley. To reach Cathedral Valley Road, follow State Route 24 east of the visitor's center for about 15 miles and turn north on the unpaved road. Access is also provided from an unpaved road at Caineville, about 7 miles farther east.

Access to the southern two-thirds of the park is provided by an unpaved road—called the Notom-Bullfrog Road—that begins about 1 mile east of the eastern park boundary on State Route 24. This road continues south all the way to Bullfrog Marina in Glen Canyon National Recreation Area. Technically, most of the road is outside of the park, on BLM land, but it provides spectacular views of the Waterpocket Fold as the massive formation rises from the surrounding desert. There is a campground inside the park at Cedar Mesa (north of Bitter Creek Divide), and south of Cedar Mesa you can take Burr Trail Road west over the Waterpocket Fold into the Escalante country (some of which is now part of the

Grand Staircase-Escalante National Monument) and, eventually, to Boulder, Utah.

Capitol Reef National Park is the best place in the world to see a monocline—a fold of layered rocks that creates an escarpment or reeflike formation. Everywhere you see how the more resistant rocks have formed domes, buttes, towers, and pinnacles as the softer rock has been eroded around them. The Temple of the Sun in Cathedral Valley is a perfect example of this process. The numerous water-pockets in the monocline are actually potholes carved by water erosion in the sandstone—these provide important sources of water for the local desert wildlife, from ravens to reptiles, bobcats to bighorns. Aerial flights over the area—available from Page, Arizona, or Moab, Utah—provide a sense of the breathtaking topography associated with a monocline.

DAYS IN THE FIELD:

CEDAR BREAKS NATIONAL MONUMENT

❖

Come on in. The earth, like the sun, like the air,

belongs to everyone—and to no one.

EDWARD ABBEY, "Come on In," *The Journey Home: Some Words in
Defense of the American West* (1977)

*C*edar Breaks National Monument (6,154 acres) is a smaller version of Bryce Canyon National Park (36,835 acres) located
about 20 miles east of Cedar City, Utah (via State Route 14). If you
are driving on Interstate 15 and don't have the time to drive all the
way to Bryce Canyon, then Cedar Breaks is definitely the place to go.
In fact, many believe the sandstone formations at Cedar Breaks are
actually brighter than those at Bryce Canyon. Both are high-altitude
parks, and consequently you will find a short season (snow lingers to
Memorial Day and sometimes falls as early as September) at Cedar
Breaks. As with Bryce Canyon, there are forests of spruce and fir,
as well as an immense amphitheater of pink and orange pinnacles
eroded from the sandstone escarpment.

The monument offers a limited amount of services compared to Bryce Canyon. There is a 5-mile scenic drive, a 30-site campground (open from June until the snow flies again), as well as a visitor's center and two developed trails (my favorite is the Wasatch Ramparts Trail, which follows the rim to Spectra Point). One of the best times to visit Cedar Breaks is late September when the aspen begin to turn—there are some wonderful photographic possibilities. Cedar Breaks is definitely more varied in color than Bryce Canyon and also has a slightly different geological appearance (fewer pinnacles and more eroded cliffs). If possible, you should visit both. I should also add that the monument offers premier cross-country skiing in winter.

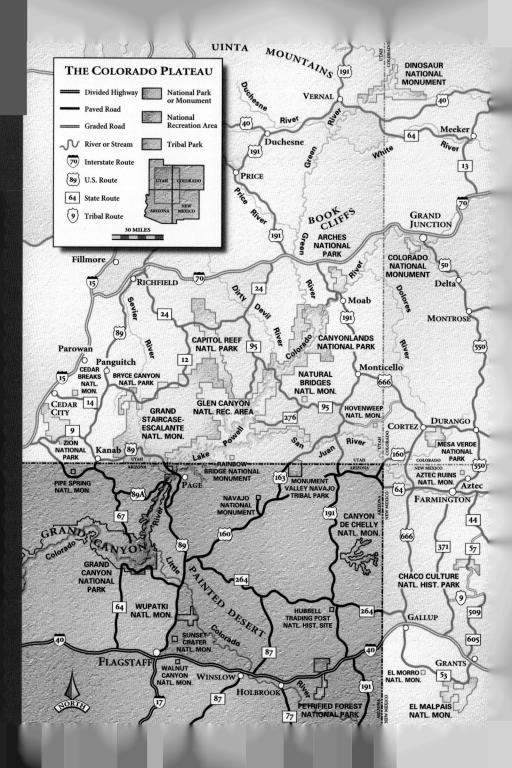

THE COLORADO PLATEAU

Divided Highway
Paved Road
Graded Road
River or Stream
Interstate Route
U.S. Route
State Route
Tribal Route

National Park or Monument
National Recreation Area
Tribal Park

30 MILES

UTAH · COLORADO

ARIZONA · NEW MEXICO

UINTA MOUNTAINS

DINOSAUR NATIONAL MONUMENT

VERNAL

Duchesne River
Green River
White River
MEEKER

Duchesne

PRICE

Price River

BOOK CLIFFS

GRAND JUNCTION

ARCHES NATIONAL PARK

COLORADO NATIONAL MONUMENT

DELTA

Fillmore

RICHFIELD

Sevier River

Dirty Devil River

Moab

Green River

Colorado River

Dolores River

MONTROSE

Parowan

Panguitch

CAPITOL REEF NATL. PARK

CANYONLANDS NATIONAL PARK

CEDAR BREAKS NATL. MON.

BRYCE CANYON NATL. PARK

Monticello

NATURAL BRIDGES NATL. MON.

CEDAR CITY

GLEN CANYON NATL. REC. AREA

GRAND STAIRCASE-ESCALANTE NATL. MON.

HOVENWEEP NATL. MON.

CORTEZ

DURANGO

ZION NATIONAL PARK

Kanab

Lake Powell

San Juan River

MESA VERDE NATIONAL PARK

AZTEC RUINS NATL. MON.

AZTEC

PIPE SPRING NATL. MON.

PAGE

RAINBOW BRIDGE NATIONAL MONUMENT

MONUMENT VALLEY NAVAJO TRIBAL PARK

FARMINGTON

NAVAJO NATIONAL MONUMENT

CANYON DE CHELLY NATL. MON.

GRAND CANYON

Colorado River

Little Colorado River

PAINTED DESERT

CHACO CULTURE NATL. HIST. PARK

GRAND CANYON NATIONAL PARK

WUPATKI NATL. MON.

HUBBELL TRADING POST NATL. HIST. SITE

GALLUP

SUNSET CRATER NATL. MON.

FLAGSTAFF

WALNUT CANYON NATL. MON.

WINSLOW

HOLBROOK

River

GRANTS

EL MORRO NATL. MON.

NORTH

PETRIFIED FOREST NATIONAL PARK

EL MALPAIS NATL. MON.

NORTHERN
ARIZONA

THE RIVER OF RETURNING:

GRAND CANYON NATIONAL PARK

❖

We are now ready to start on our way down the Great Unknown.

Our boats, tied to a common stake, chafe each other as they are

tossed by the fretful river. . . . We are three quarters of a mile in the

depths of the earth. . . . We have an unknown distance yet to run, an

unknown river to explore. What falls there are, we know not; what

rocks beset the channel, we know not, what walls rise over the river,

we know not. Ah, well! we may conjecture many things. The men talk

as cheerfully as ever; jests are bandied about freely this morning.

JOHN WESLEY POWELL, journal entry, August 13, 1969,
The Exploration of the Colorado River and Its Canyons (1874)

*T*he first bill to create a Grand Canyon National Park was introduced in 1882 by Benjamin Harrison, then a senator from
Indiana. The old Civil War general admired what his former com-
mander, Ulysses S. Grant, had done with Yellowstone in 1872 and,
being a loyal Republican and a good soldier, wanted to follow
this new national policy. Harrison's bill failed, as first bills often do.
In 1889, though, Benjamin Harrison became president and soon
proclaimed fifteen forest reserves totaling more than 13 million
acres, the Grand Canyon among them. A few years later another
Republican president and war hero, Theodore Roosevelt, visited
the place and, not to be outdone by his predecessors, on January
11, 1908, established by proclamation the Grand Canyon National
Monument.

Sunrise, Grand Canyon National Park

Theodore Roosevelt took this action under the authority of the Antiquities Act of 1906 (designed to protect archaeological sites like Mesa Verde). Many at the time questioned his authority in making such a large withdrawal from the public domain based on such a liberal interpretation of a minor act. Roosevelt, though, was intimately familiar with the oldest political axiom—power is not what is given to you, power is what you take. In one of the ironies of American history, it was President Woodrow Wilson, Roosevelt's greatest political adversary, who signed the bill giving national park status to the Grand Canyon on February 26, 1919. Various additions over the years have brought the park to its present size of 1,218,375 acres (1,903 square miles).

The Grand Canyon has changed little since the days of Major Powell, whose chronicle of adventure so electrified the American consciousness, except in one respect. The Colorado River no longer runs wild and free at the bottom. Why? In 1963 the Army Corps of Engineers built Glen Canyon Dam upstream from Lee's Ferry, impounding the snowmelt of the Rockies to form Lake Powell in what is today Glen Canyon National Recreation Area. As a result, the annual spring floods, which for millions of years were so intrinsic to the canyon, no longer occur. In the natural scheme of things, these floodwaters were, as the authors of a January 1997 *Scientific American* article stated, the "principal force sculpting the river corridor ... [depositing] sandbars and [plucking] boulders out of rapids."

On March 26, 1996, Bruce Babbitt, the former governor of Arizona and current Secretary of the Interior, reversed the post-dam situation by opening the four giant "jet tubes" at Glen Canyon Dam. Over the next week nearly one billion cubic meters of water poured through the Grand Canyon. A crew of scientists who floated the river a week later were stunned by what they saw—fresh beaches with deep sand had replaced the previously shrunken shorelines, out-of-control exotic vegetation like tamarisk had been blasted away, rock-clogged river channels were freed of their debris, rapids were widened, backwater channels were rejuvenated, and riverine wildlife habitats were restored.

In a few centuries, accumulated sand and silt will fill Lake Powell and the dam will be, from an energy and water conservation standpoint, dead. Until that time the canyon, which is a living entity as

Sunset, Grand Canyon National Park

much as we are, will have to be satisfied with these periodic controlled releases.

Most of you, of course, will not make it to the bottom of the canyon. The vast majority of visitors are content to stand at the rim and peer into the canyon or to hike down a few hot and dusty miles on one of the popular trails. A trip to the bottom is a serious matter, requiring a backpacking permit and proper gear, not to mention considerable physical stamina. A rafting trip is an even more ambitious undertaking. In making your plans—the Grand Canyon is the one place you do not want to visit without having some sort of a plan—you will have to consider the following: How much time am I going to have? In that time do I want to focus on the rim or the canyon? Do I want to visit both the South Rim and the North Rim, or do I want to concentrate on one side of the canyon? Do I want a special adventure—a mule trip, canyon overflight, or rafting trip? Do I want to stay in a cabin, a hotel room, or a campground? What trails are best for a short visit, or a longer visit?

The following two sections will help you in making those decisions.

CHANGE THE UNCHANGING:

THE SOUTH RIM OF THE GRAND CANYON

❖

I want to ask you to do one thing in connection with the Grand

Canyon in your own interest and in the interest of

the country. . . . Leave it as it is. You cannot improve on it.

The ages have been at work on it, and man can only mar it.

PRESIDENT THEODORE ROOSEVELT, standing on the rim (1903)

For over a century tourism has been a shaping force on the South Rim of the Grand Canyon. In the early years, visitors took horse-drawn wagons from Flagstaff to visit the South Rim. Eventually preexisting canyon trails used by Indians and prospectors were widened and improved to accommodate horse pack trains. By the turn of the century people were regularly taking horse pack trips down Bright Angel Trail to Indian Gardens, a natural oasis formerly used by the Anasazi and Havasupai. In 1901 the Santa Fe Railway was built from Williams, Arizona, 65 miles north to the South Rim. In 1905 the Babbitt Brothers Trading Company began a tent business on the South Rim—the company now operates the lodges, retail shops, and other visitor services on the South Rim. Two years later

The South Rim near Lipan Point, Grand Canyon National Park

the first tourist camp was established at what later became Phantom Ranch at the bottom of the canyon. In 1905 the Fred Harvey Company completed the El Tovar Hotel at the South Rim. Not long after, Theodore Roosevelt rode down Bright Angel Trail and stopped at Phantom Ranch on his way to the North Rim to hunt mountain lions. Another popular figure of the time, novelist and outdoorsman Zane Grey, would later make similar trips.

During the 1920s the Fred Harvey Company began developing tourist accommodations in earnest. It was during this decade that the rustic cabins were built at Phantom Ranch. The 1930s saw many new developments, including construction of the Desert View Watchtower in 1932 and increased trail and road building by the Civilian Conservation Corps. The paved South Rim Drive was an important addition to the park, as automobiles could course up and down the rim, stopping at various turnoffs to admire the views. One of the many to visit the South Rim in the 1930s and 1940s was photographer Ansel Adams, whose photographs of the canyon were exhibited at galleries and museums in New York and Washington.

As a result of all this history, your visit to the South Rim should proceed without difficulty. The infrastructure to support your stay is remarkable—the best of any national park in the system. Although you will not be alone—5 million people visit the Grand annually—there will be plenty of opportunity for you to get off the beaten path and have that special moment alone with the Canyon.

Driving north from Flagstaff on U.S. 180, you will pass Tusayan (camping and services available) in the national forest south of the park boundary. Once in the park you will shortly encounter Grand Canyon Village, which is the center of activities on the South Rim. There is everything here—luxury lodges (some of which are actually perched on the rim of the canyon), restaurants, gift shops, a general store, a health center, a pharmacy, a museum, a gasoline station, a photo processing shop, mule and horse corrals, a campground with 320 sites, an RV park with 84 hookup sites, an amphitheater, a bank, and a post office.

Not to mention a fine visitor's center.

From Grand Canyon Village there are two scenic drives. The West Rim Drive is closed to automobiles for most of the year—shuttles

The Palisades of the Grand Canyon,
Grand Canyon National Park

are available. The East Rim Drive, which proceeds 23 miles to Desert View, is open to automobiles and offers shuttles as well. There is a second campground on East Rim Drive at Desert View with 26 sites scattered among the pinyons and junipers, as well as a general store, gift shop, restaurant, and stone watchtower.

Where are the best views?

They are all good. Pull into any turnout along the road or, better yet, walk the Rim Trail and you will have all the great views you can photograph.

Having said that, let me also say that, in my experience, the best views of the *river* are from Lipan Point about 20 miles east of Grand Canyon Village on East Rim Drive. Here you have a penetrating view as the river enters the Inner Gorge—a photograph best shot in the early morning before the sun rises too far and the light goes flat on everything (no dramatic shadows to accentuate the dramatic geology). Navajo Mountain—nearly 100 miles distant—is visible from Lipan Point, as are the Vermillion Cliffs near Page, Arizona.

High noon on the canyon, Grand Canyon National Park

If you have a short stay—one to three days—let me recommend the following. I will assume that you are staying at Grand Canyon Village or Tusayan. The first day I would reserve for general orientation—visit the village at your leisure, read the brochures, and educate yourself more fully about the resources available. In the afternoon walk the Rim Trail that extends west from Mather Point in the village to Hermits Rest. This will be an opportunity for you to acclimatize to the high elevation and prepare yourself, if only psychologically, for a hike into the canyon—the steepness can be a bit unnerving. On the second day I would hike down one of the South Rim trails—Bright Angel, South Kaibab, Hermit, Grandview—about 2 or 3 miles, depending on your physical condition. This will give you a sense of the natural history below the rim, especially of the bands of geological history through which you will be passing. On the last day I would concentrate on photography, having acquired more of an aesthetic sense of the canyon and its moods, which change depending on the hour of the day.

A number of variations can be made on this theme, such as arranging for a mule trip down the Bright Angel Trail to Indian Gardens (check at Apache Stables) or climbing aboard a sightseeing plane for a sunset trip (check at the El Tovar Hotel) or bicycling along West Rim Drive (bike rentals not currently available).

For the handicapped, wheelchair-accessible tours are available (contact any lodge).

If I had more time—five or more days—I would look into an overnight mule or backpacking trip all the way to Phantom Ranch (reserve either in advance), an extended float trip down the Colorado River through the Grand Canyon, or a trip to Havasu Canyon on the nearby Havasupai Reservation (see Practical Information). Those with a significant interest in the natural history of the canyon should contact the Grand Canyon Field Institute (see Practical Information). Their season, which begins in mid-March and runs through the end of November, includes guided day hikes, guided backpacking trips, river trips, van camping, and classroom instruction. Their offerings are simply superb.

If you are like me, you will be back, again and again!

Distances from Grand Canyon's South Rim Village to:

Albuquerque, New Mexico . . . . 407 miles

Amarillo, Texas . . . . 674 miles

Bryce Canyon National Park, Utah . . . . 310 miles

Canyon de Chelly National Monument . . . . 243 miles

Death Valley National Park, California . . . . 440 miles

Denver, Colorado, via Cortez . . . . 649 miles

Flagstaff, Arizona, via U.S. 180 . . . . 78 miles

Four Corners Monument (U.S. 160 between Cortez, Colorado, and Kayenta, Arizona) . . . . 222 miles

Kayenta, Arizona . . . . 157 miles

Las Vegas, Nevada . . . . 290 miles

Los Angeles, California . . . . 556 miles

Mesa Verde National Park . . . . 303 miles

North Rim, Grand Canyon National Park . . . . 215 miles

Page, Arizona . . . . 140 miles

Petrified Forest National Park . . . . 189 miles

Phoenix, Arizona . . . . 220 miles

Tucson, Arizona . . . . 344 miles

Zion National Park . . . . 272 miles

THE LAST GOOD COUNTRY: THE NORTH
RIM OF THE GRAND CANYON

❖

I spent four sweet summers on that sublime North Rim. . . .
Four summers. Sweet and bitter, bittersweet hilarious seasons in
the forest of ponderosa and spruce and fir and trembling aspen
trees. The clang of horseshoes in the twilight. The smell of
woodsmoke from the cabin. Deep in the darkling pines the
flutesong of a hermit thrush. Lightning, distant thunder, and
clouds that towered into evening. Rain on the roof in the night.

EDWARD ABBEY, "Fire Lookout," *The Best of Edward Abbey* (1984)

Each spring for six years I taught a little course in nonfiction at the
University of Alaska and each spring, along about April, my
students and I would listen to a cassette tape of Edward Abbey
reading his essay "Fire Lookout." His deep sonorous voice filled the
windowless crypt of a classroom and transported us all to a sunny
special place far from the late spring blizzards of the north country.
Abbey lived in a cabin on the North Rim for four summers and came
to know the territory well. I would highly recommend either the
essay or the audiotape if you are contemplating a trip. No one ever
wrote as powerfully or as lyrically about the unique natural wonder-
land that is the North Rim.

There are four things you should know about the North Rim.

The view from the North Rim, Grand Canyon National Park

First, the North Rim is physically remote—over 200 long and winding miles by road from the South Rim. Second, the North Rim is considerably higher than the South Rim (over 8,000 feet), which means lots of snow for cross-country skiers in the winter and a season that runs only from May 15 through October 15. Third, because the North Rim is so far removed from the interstate grid, it only sees about one-tenth the number of visitors as the South Rim. Fourth, although the North Rim does not offer the spectacular river views of the South Rim because the rim is too far back from the river, you will find cross-canyon views that are just as spectacular.

To reach the northern half of the national park, turn off U.S. 89 at Jacob Lake, Arizona (great bakery with excellent blueberry and poppy muffins fresh cooked every morning), and drive south on State Route 67 for about an hour (if you're in a hurry) through a magnificent forest of quaking aspen, Douglas fir, and, chiefly, ponderosa pine. You will see mule deer here, even in the middle of the day. A few miles past Kaibab Lodge is the entrance to the national park. Another 10 miles bring you to Grand Canyon Lodge, where you will find many of the visitor services—from rustic cabins in the woods to an 82-site campground—available on the South Rim at Grand Canyon Village, though on a reduced scale because of the shorter season.

As on the South Rim, there is a nice road system along the North Rim. One of the best drives leads east of Grand Canyon Lodge to Point Imperial, Vista Encantada, the Walhalla Overlook, and Cape Royal. From Cape Royal you are about 10 miles due north of Moran Point (named for the artist Thomas Moran) on the South Rim, but to get there by road you would have to drive over 200 miles.

If you don't have much time (like only half a day), walk out to Bright Angel Point and take in the view—those snowy mountains far to the south are the San Francisco Peaks north of Flagstaff and the deep canyon just below the viewpoint is Roaring Springs Canyon. A short drive to Point Imperial (11 miles from Grand Canyon Lodge) will bring you to the highest point on either the North or South Rim—the view to the east is superb.

Those with a couple of days, or more, can take a more extensive hike along the rim trails (those cute squirrels with tufted ears are called Kaibab squirrels), thoroughly explore all the turnoffs along East Rim Drive, and contemplate taking a longer hike into the canyon.

The only maintained trail into the canyon on the North Rim is the North Kaibab Trail, which links Grand Canyon Lodge with Phantom Ranch at the bottom of the canyon. The last time I hiked on the trail—June 1996—it was glorious. As I descended through the aspen grove at the rim, a hermit thrush was singing—most beautiful birdsong in the American West—and the early morning light was streaming through the trees. The wild rose and raspberry bushes were covered with flowers and sweetened the air. Down the trail I fairly flew (you always feel like you are in great shape in the Grand Canyon, at least on the way down) through the last of the high forest, past the bright white Coconino sandstone, and through the Supai Tunnel into the zone of hot desert shrub. Miles later, at Roaring Spring, I stopped for lunch and then turned back for the long hot climb back to the surface of the planet.

At the Supai Tunnel an incident occurred which I will relate.

As I was resting near the tunnel with some other people—it is a convenient stopping place—a string of horseback riders appeared from below. The horses were tied to posts, and the riders dismounted and came over for a drink of water. There were two wranglers—a man of around fifty with a face sunburned like a piece of weathered red sandstone and a woman of indefinite age who had somehow managed to fit herself into a pair of blue jeans. Both wore sharp spurs on their cowboy boots and carried quirts tied around their wrists—riding whips with short handles and rawhide lashes. As the dozen or so horses watched their riders gather at the fountain and drink, they became visibly agitated. The horses, after all, were more thirsty than the riders. One in particular—the mount of the female wrangler—was beside himself with indignation. He was the equestrian version of Spartacus, the leader of the Roman slave rebellion. He began to throw his head around and strike the ground at regular intervals with his right hoof.

"Quit!" his rider commanded.

No effect.

"Quit, I said!"

Delivered in a shriek.

At this point she stomped over and began to beat the horse with the quirt, striking him with hard strokes about the shoulders, neck, and head.

After a minute of this, with no end in sight, the horse drew back, broke its reins free, and reared up to its full height of nine or ten feet.

The wrangler at this point turned, slipped in the mud, fell on her posterior, and slid down the hill as if on a waterslide into the small stagnant pool near the drinking fountain.

Before she could get up, the horse took off at a measured trot up the trail.

"Get back here you son of a——. Get back before I——."

Epithets such as I have not heard since my Marine Corps days.

An Israeli couple quickly herded their children into the tunnel, keeping the lesson in vernacular English as brief as possible.

The other wrangler (her father? her probation officer? both?) quietly supervised the remainder of the operation, and after awhile they left, the woman wrangler bringing up the rear on foot.

"I'll kill him," she muttered. "I swear to god I'll kill him."

Moral of the story? There is none. It is simply one small moment in the life of the canyon, another small grain in its long and lively history, preserved herein as the canyon sometimes preserves an interesting fossil in its rock.

An added feature on the North Rim is 650,000-acre Kaibab National Forest. Because of years of logging, there are many miles of old dirt roads in the forest (which is over 650,000 acres). There are also two wilderness areas in the forest—Kanab Creek (68,340 acres) and Saddle Mountain (40,610 acres). Information on the forest can be had at the park visitor's center or at the Forest Service office

North Kaibab Trail above the Redwall, Grand Canyon National Park

in Fredonia west of Jacob Lake. I must warn you that some of these roads are in variable condition, especially early in the season, and after a summer thunderstorm they can become impassable. Another problem are the rocks—there are rocks the size of tank mines and as sharp as Nordic axe-heads scattered diabolically on these backcountry roads—you don't want to get a flat with one of those dinky little factory spares when you're 40 miles from a paved road, so drive carefully if you venture into these primitive areas. On

Sunset from the North Rim, Grand Canyon National Park

the other hand, these roads are perfect for mountain bikers, who can easily avoid such obstacles and are restricted to paved roads in the parks and monuments.

What I always remember most of the North Rim is the wind, which comes from far away and breaks forever against the rocks, fresh and cool, like the breeze at the seashore. The gusts arrive in waves, then subside for a moment, then rise again, with the energy and rhythm of surf. They put the whole plant world in motion so that the rim of the canyon seems to vibrate with life. The only thing that refuses to move, other than the rocks, are the ponderosas, tall coniferous behemoths that stand heavily and at a distance from each other, like the fallen gods of Keats's *Hyperion*. In the spring their sap gathers on the blond wood like honey and sweetens the air with the fragrance of a newly built cabin.

There is the sense on the North Rim of a place that is eternally young, that will never age or be diminished, at least in the microscopic span of time allotted to the human race.

And so we keep returning, as I will the day after I mail the manuscript of this book to the publisher, for it is May and the world is young again.

FROM THE FARAWAY NEARBY:

CANYON DE CHELLY NATIONAL MONUMENT

❖

We . . . had two spectacular, stormy days in Canyon de Chelly.

I photographed the White House Ruins from almost the

identical spot and time of the O'Sullivan picture!

Can't wait until I see what I got.

ANSEL ADAMS, letter to Beaumont and Nancy Newhall (1941)

There is much history here. First there were the Anasazi, who lived in Canyon de Chelly from around 350 A.D. to around 1300 A.D. and left extensive cliff dwellings and rock art. Then came the Navajo, who moved in sometime after 1700 A.D. with their hogans and sheep and rich mythology—Spider Rock is the legendary home of Spider Woman who taught the Navajos how to weave. Finally came the Euroamericans—the Spanish, who killed Navajos, including women and children, at Massacre Cave in Canyon del Muerto in 1805, and the Americans, who in 1864, under the direction of Kit Carson, forced the Navajos to leave the area and relocate at Fort Sumner, where they lived in exile for four years. Later various government expeditions passed through, and with them

View from the trail to the White House Ruins,
Canyon de Chelly National Monument

the landscape photographers, including Timothy O'Sullivan, whose image of the White House Ruins so inspired Ansel Adams. Georgia O'Keeffe came out for a visit with Ansel Adams on one occasion, and Philip Hyde and many other prominent painters and photographers have followed.

Canyon de Chelly is one of the most stunning and inspiring places in the American landscape. Most of the distinctive red-orange cliffs are de Chelly sandstone, which dates back about 200 million years. They are particularly dramatic in the Inner Canyon around the White House Ruins, perhaps the most striking feature of the monument. At the bottom of the canyon is a meandering stream that has its origins in the Chuska Mountains to the east and ends in Chinle Wash to the west. On occasion the stream is a raging torrent, at other times it is buried beneath the sand. But it is enough for the Navajo who still live in the canyons, supporting their irrigated fields of corn and squash, their flocks of sheep, and their orchards of peaches and apples. The Navajo generally leave the canyon in the winter when it becomes cold and a more extensive fuel supply can be found on the mesa woodlands.

Canyon de Chelly National Monument is accessed from Chinle,

about 70 miles south of Four Corners on U.S. 191. Chinle offers the full range of visitor support services in terms of motels and restaurants—it is a major city for the reservation. Once you arrive at the monument you will find that there are two scenic auto tours—the South Rim and the North Rim. Most people take the South Rim, which provides access to the White House Ruins (the only location in the monument to which you may hike without a Navajo guide). The South Rim drive, which begins at the visitor's center, features a number of excellent turnouts. At mile 2.5 is the Tsegi Turnout, where you may view a hogan, the traditional eight-sided Navajo home. About 1.5 miles farther is the Junction Overlook, which provides a view of a fifteen-room cliff dwelling at the junction of Canyon del Muerto and Canyon de Chelly.

The parking lot for the trail to the White House Ruins is at mile 6.4. The trail begins about 150 yards to the right of the overlook and leads 1.25 miles down some steep rocks to the bottom of the canyon. There are many places to take photographs on this beautiful hike. If you've come this far, I strongly urge you to take the time—a couple of hours—to see the famous White House Ruins up close. They are particularly beautiful in late October, when the giant cottonwoods along the stream turn bright yellow. If you have small children, please take them by the hand on this trail, which is quite steep in places and negotiates some potentially dangerous stretches of slickrock. It also passes through a tunnel blasted through the rock at one point, which the kids will love.

At mile 21.8 from the visitor's center is another incredible site—Spider Rock (Speaking Rock can also be seen from the overlook). A number of Anasazi ruins are visible from this point, though it helps to have a pair of binoculars to spot them. Far out on the horizon above the canyon you'll see Black Rock, which, like Shiprock, is the core of an extinct volcano.

The North Rim drive features such sites as the Antelope House Overlook, the Mummy Cave Overlook, and the Massacre Cave overlook.

You will notice, particularly in the vicinity of the White House Ruins, that Navajo sell their jewelry and crafts on outstretched blankets. Always remember to be generous—your purchases bring much-needed cash to a very poor area.

If you are more adventuresome, you might want to check at the Thunderbird Lodge in Chinle or at the visitor's center for a back-country hiking or four-wheel-drive trip with a Navajo guide. Numerous rock panels with petroglyphs and remote ruins can be observed on such a trip. You also get to spend more time with the local people, which is always an advantage when traveling.

Whenever I visit Canyon de Chelly, I always think the same thing—why don't I just fall in love with a dark-haired, beautiful-eyed Navajo woman and live down there in a hogan, far from that other world? Cities may be concentrated centers of human creativity, bright and busy and full of dreams and expectations, but, for me at least, the natural faraway represented in places like Canyon de Chelly always beckons, and there is not a day that the outback does not come near. It is an old dream, the dream of finding a peaceful quiet life close to nature and living among a people for whom the industrial civilization we often blindly embrace is a pretty hilarious joke. Rousseau knew about that impulse. So did the Greeks who were his mentors. So did Abbey, whose essay on Havasu Canyon in *Desert Solitaire* explores just that possibility.

Places like Canyon de Chelly and Havasu Canyon show us an older and richer way of life, a pathway from birth to death that has the blue sky as its roof and the red desert as its floor, as opposed to acoustic tiles overhead and linoleum underfoot. Here are villages and place names from another language, another culture, another cosmology: Teec Nos Pos, Deennehotso, Lukachukai, Klagetoh, Naschitti. Here are a people who still practice the old ways of planting melons and corn, and hunting the deer, and telling the tales of Coyote and Raven. Here are people whose way of life, if nothing else, reminds us of what is important (family, nature, the imagination) and what is not.

A VERY LONG TIME AGO:

PETRIFIED FOREST NATIONAL PARK

❖

All around the margin of the valley of the Little Colorado,

on the side next to the Zuni Pueblo and on the side next to the

San Francisco Plateau, every creek and every brook runs in

a beautiful canyon. . . . Still farther down we come to the

bad lands of the Painted Desert.

JOHN WESLEY POWELL, *The Exploration of the Colorado River
and Its Canyons* (1874)

*M*ost people see the Petrified Forest, and the Painted Desert of
which it is a part, from 6 or 7 miles up on a cross-country
flight. The pilot comes on the intercom and directs the attention of
the bored and restless passengers on board to the extraordinary pal-
ette of colors on Earth below. A reverent silence fills the plane as
grandfatherly necks crane and temporarily pacified children peer. A
lucky few view the incredible spectacle from the ground. The colors
of the eroded sand hills—yellow, orange, green, black, red, purple,
pink, blue—are like the colors of the petrified wood that is found in
abundance everywhere in the park.

Petrified Forest National Park—about 115 miles east of Flagstaff,
Arizona, on Interstate 40—was established as a national monument
in 1906 by President Theodore Roosevelt. It became a national park
in 1962. The northern part of the park protects a small but dramatic part of the Painted Desert—a spectacular region of colorful

buttes, mesas, and badlands. There are a number of turnouts on the park road near the visitor's center from which these features may be viewed: Tiponi Point, Tawa Point, Kachina Point, Chinle Point, Pintado Point, Nizhoni Point, Whipple Point, and Lacey Point. From the road and to the north, across the black forest and Lithodendron Wash, distinctive Chinle Mesa is visible. Toward the northwest, over Digger Wash, is Pilot Rock. The Painted Desert area is particularly beautiful in the summer following a rare desert thunderstorm, when the brightness of the hues in the sediment is accentuated by the moisture.

On the road to the south visitors will find such features as the Puerco Indian Ruin, Newspaper Rock (an outstanding panel of native rock art), and Blue Mesa. Petrified trees literally litter the ground in this portion of the park, and there are a number of outstanding turnouts: Agate Bridge, Jasper Forest, Crystal Forest, The Flattops, and Agate House. At the Rainbow Forest Museum, just north of U.S. 181, various specimens may be observed. The Park Service has a problem with people illegally carting off samples of petrified wood—please do not add to this national disgrace. Rangers will gladly direct you to legitimate commercial dealers who collect specimens outside the park and offer them for sale.

There is no developed campground in the park—cross-country hiking possibilities and backpack camping are available. Obtain permits from the rangers at the visitor's center.

Each time I visit the Petrified Forest I think of the old Humphrey Bogart–Bette Davis movie, *The Petrified Forest,* that appeared in 1936 and helped to launch both their acting careers. The film was based on the acclaimed Robert Sherwood Broadway play and includes some great lines, as when Bette Davis, swept up by the beauty of the Painted Desert, exclaims to Leslie Howard (the actor who played Ashley Wilkes in *Gone with the Wind*), "We've been fighting nature for too long! We've got to learn to get along with her!" These lines were quite resonant in 1936, when the Great Plains had been turned into a desert by the rapine agricultural practices of the time.

THE DESERT AS ART: HUBBELL TRADING

POST NATIONAL HISTORICAL SITE

❖

There was no Sun or Moon, but the mountains gave light.

Navajo creation myth

*T*he tradition of the Indian trading post, so strongly associated with the Four Corners region of the Colorado Plateau, is well preserved in the Hubbell Trading Post National Historic Site, whose profits go to the national parks system. Here you may find jewelry, baskets, pottery, blankets, sand paintings, and other Navajo artworks and crafts. Nearby is the original Hubbell home (circa 1900), which features some nice Maynard Dixon paintings (an important landscape painter of the Southwest). Anyone interested in trading posts and galleries in the Four Corners region should refer to Patrick Eddington and Susan Makov's definitive *Trading Post Guidebook* (Northland, 1995).

The post is about 40 miles south of Chinle, Arizona (Canyon de Chelly National Monument), via U.S. 191 and State Route 264. The nearest reservation town is Ganado, and the nearest large community is Gallup, New Mexico.

THE DESERT SUBLIME:

MONUMENT VALLEY NAVAJO TRIBAL PARK

❖

Scattered over [this desert] are many castle-like buttes

and slender towers, none of which can be less than 1,000 feet

in height, their sides absolutely perpendicular, their forms

wonderful imitations of the structures of human art. . . .

we could hardly resist the conviction that we beheld the walls

and towers of some Cyclopean city hitherto undiscovered

in this faroff region.

JOHN NEWBERRY, *Navajo Wildlands* (1859)

*M*onument Valley is one of the most extraordinary landscapes on the continent. Even if you have seen the famous soaring shafts of stone in a dozen biblical and Western movies, the first glimpse of the magnificent city of rock will still amaze. Driving on the blacktop south of Mexican Hat, Utah (where I usually spend the night at the Navajo Inn), I always pull over at the Redlands Viewpoint to take in the panorama. To the south and west are the Mitten Buttes. Due south is Rooster Rock. Various other standing pedestals, terraced mesas, and upright pinnacles are scattered about the country like the colossal handcarved pieces of some game board of the gods.

And over it all magnificent clouds drift, like something out of a Maynard Dixon painting.

Movie after movie has been made in Monument Valley—from *Stagecoach* in 1938 to *How the West Was Won* in 1962 to *Back to the*

Sunrise in Monument Valley Navajo Tribal Park

Future in 1988. Undoubtedly many more will be filmed in the centuries to come.

It is a landscape of pure inspiration.

It is also a piece of territory belonging entirely to the Navajo Nation. It is the one site in this book that is not a national park or monument. Monument Valley was the first Navajo tribal park, established as such in 1958 by the tribal council. Visitors will not notice much difference—a park is a park, whether its rangers work for the federal or state government or for the Navajo Nation.

At the entrance to the park (about 45 minutes south of Mexican Hat on U.S. 163) dozens of Navajo vendors sell jewelry, sand paintings, rugs, pottery, sun-bleached cattle skulls, and food. The side road due west from the junction leads to Goulding's Monument Valley Trading Post and Lodge (John Wayne stayed here at various times from 1939 to 1964 while filming in the area). The side road due east, along which the vendors are assembled, leads into the park. At the top of the hill 1 mile past the entrance you will find the visitor's center, which includes a gift shop, and a campground area. Here there is no shortage of Navajo guides, some with jeeps or vans to take you on tours. You may also follow the self-guided valley road in your vehicle.

No one should pass through Monument Valley without visiting the vendors at the junction or touring the tribal park. If the buttes are lovely from the highway, they are overwhelming when you are among them. Imagine a collection of several dozen 100-story sky-scrapers still waiting for the smaller buildings of the city to be built around them. Or sculpted humanlike figures as tall as the Washington Monument—ridge after ridge of them. Or stone-topped natural pyramids beside which the great pyramid of Rameses would seem nothing more than the pathetic sandcastle of a bored child.

And, lest I forget, the whole scene is painted in every color of the rainbow.

A WALK IN THE SUN: PIPE SPRING

NATIONAL MONUMENT

❖

A few years ago a party of Mormons set out from St. George,
Utah, taking with them a boat, and came down to the Grand
Wash. . . . Three men—Hamblin, Miller and Crosby—taking the
boat, went on down the river to Callville, landing a few miles
below the mouth of the Rio Virgen. We have their manuscript
journal with us, and so the stream is comparatively well known.

JOHN WESLEY POWELL, *The Exploration of the Colorado River*
and Its Canyons (1874)

*P*ipe Spring National Monument, located about 10 miles west of
Fredonia, Arizona, is the most distinctive national monument
on the Colorado Plateau. This restored 20-acre ranch memorializes
and recreates Mormon pioneer life through a living-history program. During the summer, descendants of the first Mormons dress
in pioneer clothes and explain Mormon traditions to visitors. Each
September, an annual wagon ride is made from Pipe Spring to St.
George, celebrating and recreating the historic "Honeymoon Trail"
by which Mormon couples would travel to St. George to marry.

As Major Powell intimates, these early Mormon pioneers did
much to explore and uncover the secrets of the Colorado Plateau, as
with the "Arizona Strip" north of the Grand Canyon around Pipe
Spring, and posterity owes them much.

REMAINS OF THE DAY:

NAVAJO NATIONAL MONUMENT

❖

The most wonderful ruin in the Southwest is Betatakin,

in a canyon tributary to Tsegi. . . . In late afternoon, when the

sunlight reflected off the canyon walls imparts a warm

orange glow to the whole vaulted cavern the combination of light,

color and antiquity creates an atmosphere more magic than that

of any other ruin. Keet Seel, however, surpasses even Betatakin

in giving an idea of 13th century life in these canyons.

STEPHEN JETT, *Navajo Wildlands* (1967)

The ruins of Betatakin and Keet Seel, protected by Navajo National Monument, are, as Jett indicates, about as good as they come. The monument is accessed via U.S. 160 18 miles south of Kayenta.

Betatakin, which evokes the extensive Cliff Palace at Mesa Verde National Park, was built on the floor of an enormous natural alcove, the roof of which extends far above the stone cliff dwellings. At one time it had nearly 150 rooms and, like the ruins at Mesa Verde and elsewhere, was occupied through the thirteenth century A.D. The Betatakin ruin, with more than 160 rooms, is accessed via a 1-mile trail from the visitor's center. The ruins of Keet Seel though— the largest in Arizona—are quite a bit more remote and can only be accessed by horseback and in the company of a Navajo guide. Horse rentals are available at the nearby Navajo Trading Post. A third site—Inscription House (a 75-room pueblo)—is 27 miles from the visitor's center. It requires a hike of around 4 miles round-trip.

A visit to any of these sites takes you into the heart of Navajo Country, which offers some of the most spectacular scenery on the Colorado Plateau. Here you will find canyons and mesas, slickrock and sand, peaks and pinnacles, and all in the bright hues that Navajo rugs and pottery celebrate with such exhilaration.

THE GREEN FACE OF THE DESERT:

WALNUT CANYON NATIONAL MONUMENT

❖

What interests me is the quality of that pre-Columbian life,

the feel of it, the atmosphere. . . . Fear: is that the key to

their lives? What persistent and devilish enemies they must

have had, or thought they had . . . [to] make their homes,

as swallows do, in niches high on the face of a cliff.

EDWARD ABBEY, *Desert Solitaire* (1968)

*H*igh in the cliffs of Walnut Canyon there are a series of natural overhangs which today protect the ruins of over 200 single-room dwellings. These were left by the Sinagua, not the Anasazi, but the Sinagua had a lifestyle similar to the Anasazi: cliff dwellings and an agriculture built around beans, corn, and squash and the hunting of small game such as rabbits and turkeys. Some archaeologists believe the Sinagua began building their cliff houses in Walnut Canyon shortly after the volcanic eruption that created Sunset Crater just to the north (see Sunset Crater National Monument). In Walnut Canyon the Sinagua found a reliable source of water—a dam upstream now stops the flow of water—and a secure, comfortable place to live. After about 200 years the Sinagua left, in a familiar pattern, around the year 1300 A.D.

Walnut Canyon National Monument is located 9 miles east of Flagstaff on Interstate 40. There is a visitor's center, a picnic ground, and several pleasant short hikes around the ruins but no public campground.

LONG AGO AND FAR AWAY: WUPATKI AND

SUNSET CRATER NATIONAL MONUMENTS

❖

East of San Francisco Peak there is another low volcanic cone,

composed of ashes which have been slightly cemented by the

processes of time, but which can be worked with great ease. On this

cone another tribe of Indians made its village. . . . Some twelve or

fifteen miles farther east is another volcanic cone. . . . This is the

region of the Painted Desert, for the marls and soft rocks of which

the hills are composed are of many colors.

JOHN WESLEY POWELL, *The Exploration of the Colorado River*
and Its Canyons (1874)

Separated by only 10 miles, these two national monuments are among the most popular sites in the greater Flagstaff area. Both are located in the drainage of the Little Colorado River, which drains north into Grand Canyon National Park. To the east is the magnificent Painted Desert and to the west a short distance are the San Francisco Peaks, the tallest mountains in Arizona. Sunset Crater is associated with the great San Francisco Peaks volcanic field, of which 12,643-foot Humphreys Peak is the most conspicuous member. Scientists believe the volcano exploded about the time of the Battle of Hastings (1066 A.D.). All that remains today is a 1,000-foot cinder cone. Oddly enough, within a few years of the eruption the resident natives apparently returned to fields fertilized by the ash in the nearby Wupatki area and they numbered perhaps several thousand. These were the Sinagua Indians. Within Wupatki are hundreds of ruins, including a circular stone amphitheater and a prehistoric ball court like those found in Central America. The central structure of the community was three stories high and had over a hundred rooms.

Sunset Crater National Monument (3,040 acres) is 15 miles north of Flagstaff, Arizona, via U.S. 89. Wupatki National Monument (35,253 acres) is about 11 miles down the loop road from Sunset Crater and includes a visitor's center, viewpoints, and picnic area (no public campgrounds).

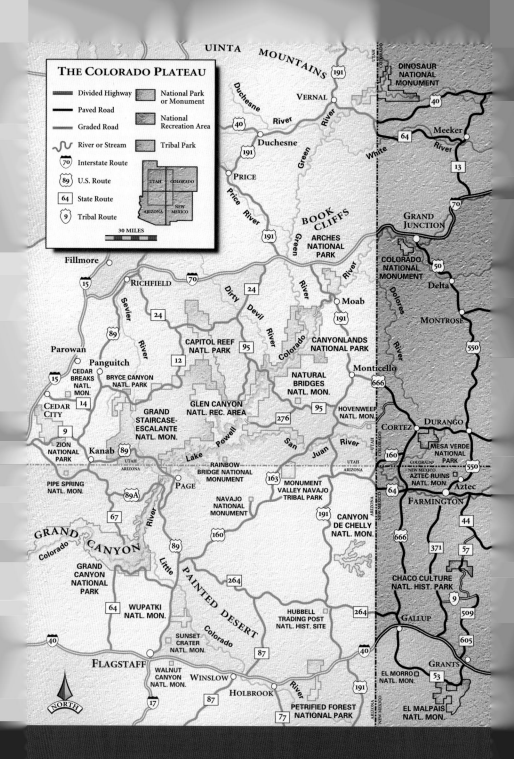

THE COLORADO PLATEAU

- ═══ Divided Highway
- ▬▬▬ Paved Road
- ═══ Graded Road
- ∿∿∿ River or Stream
- 🛡70 Interstate Route
- 🛡89 U.S. Route
- ☐64 State Route
- 🛡9 Tribal Route

National Park or Monument

National Recreation Area

Tribal Park

UTAH | COLORADO
ARIZONA | NEW MEXICO

30 MILES

UINTA MOUNTAINS

UTAH / COLORADO

DINOSAUR NATIONAL MONUMENT

Duchesne River

Green River

VERNAL

191

40

Meeker

White River

64

Meeker River

13

Duchesne

191

Price River

PRICE

Green River

BOOK CLIFFS

GRAND JUNCTION

70

ARCHES NATIONAL PARK

COLORADO NATIONAL MONUMENT

50

Delta

FILLMORE

15

RICHFIELD

70

24

Dirty Devil River

River

Colorado River

Moab

191

Dolores River

MONTROSE

550

Sevier River

24

CAPITOL REEF NATL. PARK

95

CANYONLANDS NATIONAL PARK

Monticello

666

PAROWAN

89

12

Panguitch

CEDAR BREAKS NATL. MON.

BRYCE CANYON NATL. PARK

NATURAL BRIDGES NATL. MON.

95

HOVENWEEP NATL. MON.

CORTEZ

DURANGO

Parowan

15

14

CEDAR CITY

9

GRAND STAIRCASE-ESCALANTE NATL. MON.

GLEN CANYON NATL. REC. AREA

276

MESA VERDE NATIONAL PARK

160

550

Lake Powell

San Juan River

UTAH / COLORADO

COLORADO

AZTEC RUINS NATL. MON.

Aztec

ZION NATIONAL PARK

Kanab

89

RAINBOW BRIDGE NATIONAL MONUMENT

UTAH / ARIZONA

FARMINGTON

PIPE SPRING NATL. MON.

89A

PAGE

163

MONUMENT VALLEY NAVAJO TRIBAL PARK

64

44

67

NAVAJO NATIONAL MONUMENT

191

CANYON DE CHELLY NATL. MON.

666

371

57

GRAND CANYON

Colorado River

89

160

Little Colorado River

PAINTED DESERT

264

CHACO CULTURE NATL. HIST. PARK

9

509

GRAND CANYON NATIONAL PARK

64

WUPATKI NATL. MON.

HUBBELL TRADING POST NATL. HIST. SITE

264

GALLUP

605

40

SUNSET CRATER NATL. MON.

Colorado River

87

40

GRANTS

FLAGSTAFF

WALNUT CANYON NATL. MON.

WINSLOW

Little Colorado River

EL MORRO NATL. MON.

53

17

87

HOLBROOK

77

PETRIFIED FOREST NATIONAL PARK

191

ARIZONA / NEW MEXICO

EL MALPAIS NATL. MON.

NORTH

The Land Through Which the River Runs: Dinosaur National Monument

How It Was: Mesa Verde National Park

Badlands: El Malpais and El Morro National Monuments

WESTERN COLORADO AND NORTHWESTERN NEW MEXICO

Desert Worlds: Chaco Culture National Historical Park

DESERT WORLDS: CHACO CULTURE
NATIONAL HISTORICAL PARK

❖

Perhaps the most interesting ruins of America are found

in this region. The ancient pueblos found here are of

superior structure . . . wherever there is water, near by an ancient

ruin may be found; and these ruins are gathered about centers,

the centers being larger pueblos and the scattered ruins

representing single houses.

JOHN WESLEY POWELL, *The Exploration of the Colorado River*
and Its Canyons (1874)

Sometime around 600 A.D.—about the same time as the legendary reign of King Arthur in western England—a group of people
the archaeologists call The Basketmakers began farming the fields of
Chaco Canyon (a tributary of the San Juan River). At first they lived
in pit houses, but over time they learned to build larger, and
then larger, pueblos. Eventually they constructed an enormous
rambling place, now called Pueblo Bonito ("beautiful village") that
was five stories in height, covered three acres, and included about 800
rooms—this at a time when the people of England were living in the
most primitive Dark Ages villages you can imagine. They flourished
for awhile, these good farming people of Chaco, and then, in a familiar story, vacated the place and left for parts unknown sometime

around the year 1300 A.D., probably for more reliable water sources closer to the Rio Grande.

Chaco Culture National Historical Park, which contains a dozen pueblo or village ruins, is reached via State Route 44 southeast of Farmington, New Mexico. The side road into the park is undeveloped and in times of snow or rain may be impassable—check before heading into the monument. The monument, which is roughly 4 miles by 8 miles in size, includes a visitor's center with some excellent artifacts and a campground that's a real "out in the middle of nowhere" place, which gives it much charm in my book. All around it are the lands of the Navajo Nation, and to the west the Chuska Mountains silhouette many a beautiful sunset.

Pueblo stone work, Chaco Culture
National Historical Monument

ANOTHER COUNTRY:

AZTEC RUINS NATIONAL MONUMENT

❖

Among them I walk.

I speak to them;

They hold out their hands to me.

Song of the Long Pot (Navajo)

*M*idway between Mesa Verde to the north and Chaco Canyon to the south the Anasazi maintained a village and cultivated lands known today as the Aztec Ruins and located about 1 mile north of Aztec, New Mexico, on U.S. 550. The central ruins, which are quite large—about 350 by 250 feet—consist of a quadrangle of stone rooms, which ascend to three stories in places. This area is believed to have originally had about 500 rooms and supported a population of at least 400. By far, the most impressive feature of Aztec Ruins is the great kiva, which has been well restored—with an inside diameter of 48 feet, the kiva provides a sense of how grand these ancient religious structures were in their time (the *inside* diameter of the kiva is 48 feet!). The monument maintains a small visitor's center with a museum containing Anasazi artifacts. Services can be found at Aztec.

(In this same geographic area is Yucca House National Monument, which is not covered in this book because the ruins are unexcavated at this time and the monument, which is administered by Mesa Verde National Park, is not open to the public.)

BADLANDS: EL MALPAIS AND EL MORRO
NATIONAL MONUMENTS

❖

But with the floods of lava came great explosions,

like that of Krakatoa, by which the heavens were filled

with volcanic dust.

JOHN WESLEY POWELL, *The Exploration of the Colorado River
and Its Canyons* (1874)

*I*n extreme northwestern New Mexico, near the headwaters of the
Little Rio Grande River, which drains into the Grand Canyon, are
two little visited but highly significant national monuments. El
Malpais (114,272 acres) preserves an extensive region of lava-formed
landforms: cinder cones, black lava flows, *pahoehoe* (ropelike lava),
spatter cones, lava tubes (including one of the longest known to sci-
ence), and cinder cones (1,800-foot Bandera Crater). El Malpais also
includes highland forests of ponderosa pine, Douglas fir, and quaking aspen, as well as semidesert woodlands of pinyon and juniper. Archaeological evidence—such as the famous Folsom points,
discoverd near Clovis, New Mexico, dating human occupation in this
area to the Ice Age—suggests people were living in the El Malpais
environs as long as 9,000 years ago.

El Morro National Monument, on the road to the Zuni Indian
Reservation, follows an ancient Indian trading route past a sandstone
mesa visible for miles in the desert. On the top of the mesa is an 875-
room pueblo of a mixed Anasazi and Mogollon heritage, apparently
abandoned early in the fourteenth century. At the base of the mesa

is an expanse of smooth sandstone on which Indians, Spanish conquistadors, and later travelers and explorers have left their "Kilroy was here" inscriptions. These include an inscription made by Juan de Onate in 1607 and by Diego de Vargas in 1692. Naturally it is called Inscription Rock.

Utah agave, El Morro National Monument

The El Morro visitor's center features an excellent museum.

Both national monuments are easily accessed via Interstate 40 west of Albuquerque, New Mexico. El Malpais National Monument is reached via the State Route 117 exit or the State Route 53 exit; El Morro National Monument is reached via the State Route 53 exit. An added benefit of visiting this area is that you can also stop by the incredible Acoma and Laguna Pueblos also accessed by Interstate 40. Acoma (the "Sky City") simply must be seen by anyone traveling through this area.

THE LAND THROUGH WHICH THE RIVER
RUNS: DINOSAUR NATIONAL MONUMENT

❖

Into the middle of the stream we row, and down the rapid river

we glide, only making strokes enough with the oars to guide

the boat. What a headlong ride it is! Shooting past rocks

and islands. I am soon filled with exhilaration only experienced

before in riding a fleet horse over the outstretched prairie.

One, two, three, four miles we go, rearing and plunging the waves,

until we wheel to the right into a beautiful park and land on

an island, where we go into camp.

JOHN WESLEY POWELL, journal entry, June 22, 1869,
An Exploration of the Colorado River and Its Canyons (1874)

Although Major Powell ran the Green River in 1869 through what is today Dinosaur National Monument, it was not until 1892 that dinosaur bones were first seen, and another seventeen years would pass before the rich major bed was found. This occurred in 1909, when Earl Douglas, a scientist working for the Carnegie Museum in Pittsburgh, stumbled upon an incredible scene—a unique one-of-a-kind area in which a large number of dinosaurs perished in the sand along a river backwater. By 1922 the Carnegie Museum had recovered the complete skeletal remains of twenty dinosaurs. In 1938 the original monument, which had been established in 1915, was enlarged to include over 300 square miles in northwestern Colorado and northeastern Utah. This was done not only to preserve the unusual dinosaur quarry but also to protect the canyons of the Green River—Lodore, Whirlpool, and Split Mountain—through which Major Powell had journeyed just after the Civil War. An attempt by the federal government to dam the river and flood the canyons in the 1950s was successfully defeated by environmentalists, although another dam was constructed at that time in Glen Canyon to the south.

The monument is just north of U.S. 40 on the state line. There are three primary access roads. The first—a self-guided scenic drive—proceeds north of the visitor's center, which is located on the Colorado side of the monument, and leads to Canyon Overlook, Island Park Overlook, Echo Park Overlook, and Echo Park, where there is a ranger station and a 13-site campground. The second proceeds north of Jensen, Utah (25 miles west of the visitor's center), toward the Dinosaur Quarry, the Red Rock Nature Trail, a ranger station, and two campgrounds: Split Mountain with 4 sites and Green River with 88 sites. The third, used primarily by river rafters, is accessed from State Route 318 to the north and leads to the Gates of Ladore ranger station and campground with 17 sites.

Near Gates of Lodore, Dinosaur National Monument

There is a lot to do in Dinosaur, from viewing the spectacular dinosaur bones at the quarry, to river rafting (check with monument officials for licensed outfitters), to backcountry hiking (the 5-mile trail to Ruple Point west of the Island Park Overlook provides a nice sense of the high desert country), to exploring the undeveloped roads with a four-wheel-drive (the Yampa Bench Road runs 38 miles east of Echo Park Road). Additionally, the BLM maintains a number of proposed wilderness areas in the surrounding country (see John Fielder's *Colorado BLM Wildlands* in Further Reading), including Vermillion Basin, Cold Springs Mountain, Cross Mountain, and what are referred to by government planners as the "Dinosaur National Monument Adjacent Areas." Of these I can highly recommend the one I have visited—Vermillion Basin, northeast of the Gates of Ladore.

Dinosaur National Monument is a real Jurassic Park. Paleontologists have excavated bones from a variety of reptiles, ranging from those that were the size of dogs to those that assumed the stature of jetliners. All lived, and died, about 145 million years ago, long before the first primitive mammals arose. Who knows, if an impacting meteor had not changed Earth's climate the dominant species on earth might now be a cold-blooded reptile instead of a warm-blooded mammal. Such are the vagaries and vicissitudes of life in a free, open universe in which, literally, anything can happen (the only sort of universe I'd want to inhabit).

Rugged backcountry, Dinosaur National Monument

SECRET PARADISE:

COLORADO NATIONAL MONUMENT

❖

Above and between the canyons is the slickrock benchland,

that weird world of hills, holes, humps and hollows where, they

say, the wind always blows and nothing ever grows.

EDWARD ABBEY, *Slickrock* (1971)

Colorado National Monument, in the outskirts of Grand Junction, Colorado, presents a miniature version of what you will find in Arches and Canyonlands National Parks. In the 20,454-acre monument are isolated monoliths, including Balanced Rock and Pipe Organ, deep (1,000 feet) canyons, brightly colored sandstone, fossilized dinosaur bones, ancient Native American artifacts, and the yucca-cactus and juniper-pinyon ecological communities so common across the Colorado Plateau. Hikers in the backcountry sometimes see the small herd of desert bighorn sheep that lives in the area—mule deer and coyotes are more common. The visitor's center is near the Fruita entrance just south of Interstate 70, as is the campground and picnic area. Most visitors take the 22-mile drive through the monument, which features numerous scenic turnouts.

I suppose that for many people, traveling east or west on Interstate 70, a brief stop and drive-through in Colorado National Monument is the only experience they will ever have of the Colorado Plateau. If that is the case, they will have savored, in this little microcosm, much of the larger macrocosm that extends to the south. Here is everything—in terms of form and color, geology and ecology—you will find in Glen Canyon or the Grand Canyon. A whole wonderful essay could be written on Colorado National Monument, and probably should be.

Canyon stream, Colorado National Monument

HOW IT WAS:

MESA VERDE NATIONAL PARK

❖

The Mesa Verde is a somewhat irregular table-land,

comprising an area of about seven hundred square miles. . . .

The [Mancos Canyon] seems to have been a favorite resort of the

cliff-dwelling people, and traces of their industry may be found

everywhere, along the bottoms, in the cliffs, and on the high,

dry table-lands above. . . . So cleverly are the houses hidden away

in the dark recesses, and so very like the surrounding cliffs in

color, that [on one occasion] I had almost completed [a] sketch of

[an] upper house before the lower . . . one was detected.

They are at least eight hundred feet above the river.

W. H. HOLMES, *Report on the Expedition of 1875 and 1876*

*M*esa Verde National Park protects the most extensive and best-preserved archaeological ruins north of Latin America. The Anasazi ruins in some places reach a density of 100 ruins per square mile. The park occupies a high mesa between several canyons at the headwaters of the Mancos River, a tributary of the San Juan River. Across the mesa top are numerous pueblo ruins and among the inner canyons are the larger, often hidden cliff houses. So difficult are some of these cliff houses to see that the largest one, the 217-room Cliff Palace, was not even located until 1888, fourteen years after William Henry Jackson made his historic photographic tour of

Cliff Palace Ruins, Mesa Verde National Park

the area. It was found by two ranchers—Richard Wetherill and his brother-in-law Charles Mason—out looking for cattle. Fortunately, a movement was started shortly after to give Mesa Verde (Spanish for "green mesa") federal protection. In 1906 Congress and President Theodore Roosevelt set the core of the region aside as Mesa Verde National Park.

The Anasazi were masters of using the local geology to their advantage. This is particularly evident at the Mesa Verde site, where the Anasazi found numerous alcoves—shallow, cavelike openings in the sedimentary rock—in which they could build homes, storage areas, and religious structures. There are over a dozen parallel, steep-sided side canyons along the Mancos River in this area, and in the uplands of these canyons, where alcoves are abundant, the Anasazi built their homes beneath the top layer of the mesa. These homes had every advantage: They were in protected locations beneath the level of the earth, they were difficult to see unless a person was right on them, and they were often solar-heated by virtue of their geographic position.

The Anasazi occupied this area from around 500 A.D. (Rome was falling to the barbarians back in the Old World) to around 1300 (Mel Gibson's movie *Braveheart* depicts life in England at the time). During that time the Anasazi maintained extensive fields on the mesa tops, with vast water collection and irrigation systems, and hunted deer, rabbits, squirrels, turkeys, and other small game. They made fine jewelry, baskets, and pottery, harvested nuts and berries, constructed homes, had children, buried their dead, told stories, narrated histories, invented myths, worshipped in kivas. Toward the end of the thirteenth century an extensive drought across the Southwest made life difficult for the people of Mesa Verde. Toward the end of this period, for whatever reasons, the villages at Mesa Verde, and elsewhere in the Anasazi region, were vacated. If you want to see the Anasazi today, visit the Hopi. Many scientists believe they are the descendants of the Anasazi.

Because of the large number of ruins in the park, I strongly recommend a stay of at least two days. If you have only one day, I suggest you visit the Far View Visitor's Center for general orientation (15 miles from the park entrance station) and from there proceed south over Chapin Mesa on the park road to the major assemblage of ruins at the end of the mesa: Cedar Tree Tower, Spruce Tree Tower, the Pueblo Ruins, the Sun Temple, and the Cliff Palace. Each of these can

Mesa-top stone structure, Mesa Verde National Park

be seen in turn, although all visits will of necessity be fairly short. Because most of the ruins in Mesa Verde are in west-facing cliffs, the best times for photography (in some cases, the only time for photography) are later in the afternoon, when the sun's rays fully illuminate the ruins under the rock overhangs.

If you have time for an overnight stay, you will find an excellent campground (450 sites) at Morefield Village south of the park entrance and a superb lodge opened seasonally at Far View Point, where the rooms have commanding views south into the Navajo Reservation and Four Corners region. The possibilities, given more time, are quite extensive. You can hike down into the Cliff Palace and Balcony House from Ruins Road (a .25-mile hike), explore the Far View Ruins located 1 mile south of the Far View Visitor's Center, and catch a free mini-train for the tour of the numerous sites on Wetherill Mesa, to name just several of the many wonderful possibilities.

Although much of the 52,074-acre park is restricted, there are still some opportunities for hiking. Popular trails include the Spruce Canyon Trail, which takes you on a 2-mile hike from a mesa top to a canyon floor, and the Petroglyph Point Trail, which leads 3 miles to a panel of Anasazi rock art. The Prater Ridge Trail (7.8 miles) is the longest hiking trail in the park and follows the top of Prater Ridge. Handy little trail guides on all these hikes are available at the visitor's center. As you hike through the park you will notice extensive evidence of the forest fires of the 1996 summer, which was very dry, reminding us of the drought problems once faced by the Anasazi. These fires damaged some rock panels but also exposed other sites (over ninety) that were previously hidden.

You will see wildlife occasionally as you drive and walk around the mesa, from mule deer to marmots, tarantulas to turkeys, ravens to rattlesnakes. Coyotes can often be heard yipping in the morning or evening. Turkey vultures patrol the skies, looking for carrion. Lizards dart among the rocks. The plant life is also of interest—the ubiquitous yucca was a vital plant for the Anasazi, from which they

Cliff dwelling detail, Mesa Verde National Park

got fibers to make baskets and sandals, sewing needles, soap (from the crushed roots), and food (the flowers and fruity seed pods are edible). They also harvested pinyon nuts and ate berries such as wild raspberry and strawberry as available.

A visit to Mesa Verde, especially to one of the major living areas such as Cliff Palace, reminds us of how fragile human life is, and how brief our stay on Earth is. Here children once played, and mothers sang songs, and fathers hunted for deer to feed their families. Now all that remains of their world are ruins, telling us with a power greater than mere words that life is short and death is long and that we must all do good while we can.

THE PLACE WE CAME FROM:

SOME CLOSING THOUGHTS ON THE

COLORADO PLATEAU

❖

We do not understand that life is paradise, for it suffices
only to wish to understand it, and at once paradise will appear in
front of us in all its beauty.

FYODOR DOSTOYEVSKY, *The Brothers Karamazov* (1880)

I.

In his book *The Grand Canyon of the Colorado* (1920), John Van Dyke—an art history professor at Rutgers University—asked the question "What does it mean?"

He attempted no answer and did not provide any further guidance. He simply posed the question, as a teacher should. But in the absence of an explanation, I have—for I am the eternal student—often pondered his words.

It is a good question. Perhaps too good, for it strikes at the heart of the matter, and I do mean matter.

There are two possibilities. Either the canyon—which we can take as an emblem for nature—means nothing or it means something. Edward Abbey, in his essay "Down the River," embraced the former point of view: "What does it mean? It means nothing. It is as it is and has no need for meaning. The desert lies beneath and soars beyond any possible human qualification. Therefore, sublime."

Sublime?

That response has always seemed to me inadequate. Sublime, a

Owachomo Bridge, Natural Bridges National Monument

term introduced by the Roman philosopher Longinus, means "glorious, resplendent, majestic." Something is sublime if it causes a "lifting up" (*ekstasis*) of the spirit. How does it help our understanding to simply state that the Grand Canyon, i.e., nature both wild and human, is beautiful? And, if it is beautiful—organized according to regular laws and patterns—how can it then mean nothing? Why should there be beauty—systematically arranged matter—if there is no purpose? If matter had no purpose, wouldn't the reverse be true—anarchy instead of order? Doesn't beauty prove by its very form that its existence is not without reason? And doesn't that design imply a designer?

It is much more difficult to say that nature, both wild nature and human nature, means something, because then you have to uncover that meaning.

To me the Colorado Plateau is pretty clear evidence of how powerfully change permeates the universe, indeed is the theme of the

Needles District, Canyonlands National Park

cosmos. Major Powell, writing in *The Exploration of the Colorado River and Its Canyons* (1874), expressed it this way:

> *Now we have canyon gorges and deeply eroded valleys, and still the hills are disappearing, the mountains themselves are wasting away, the plateaus are dissolving, and the geologist, in the light of the past history of the earth, makes prophecy of a time when this desolate land of Titanic rocks shall become a valley of many valleys, and yet again the sea will invade the land, and the coral animals build their reefs. . . . Thus ever the land and sea are changing; old lands are buried, and new lands are born.*

The message is clear—change pervades all that we know and can experience with a force that cannot be opposed and with a thoroughness that could be called wisdom.

Nor is there anything original about this line of thinking.

Listen to my old friend Marcus Aurelius, dead now some twenty centuries: "Observe constantly that all things take place by change, and accustom yourself to consider that the nature of the Universe loves nothing so much as to change the things which are and to make new things like them." Or his Greek mentor Heraclitus: "Everything flows and nothing abides; everything gives way and nothing stays fixed" and "It is in changing that things find repose."

Read any of the Asian philosophers—Lao-Tzu, Confucius, Mencius—and you will find the same understanding.

What, then, shall we take away with us from the rim of the canyon?

For me, it is simple—the belief that those who embrace change are liberated and those who resist are annihilated. I can live by this principle with as much trust as if I had heard it in a lecture hall from a venerated scholar. In a sense I have, for the Plateau Country is not unlike a great university—a Harvard without doors, an Oxford without dons, a Heidelberg without the hubris. There are department heads that wear the black robes of the raven, and deans with the all-seeing eyes of a desert bighorn, and lecture halls built to hold a generation. Lessons are delivered hourly, by example, on all the virtues William Bennet extols. We learn about courage in the face of adversity, and freedom and responsibility, and the price to be paid for avarice or ignorance. The library houses two billion years of history, and the outdoor museums contain the ruins of a half-dozen dead cultures. At night, the classrooms expand to include the farthest visible stars.

Let insincerity and ambition reign elsewhere. The Colorado Plateau will forever be the domain of the sun and the sand, the river and the rock, a landscape from the Book of Genesis or the mind of Thomas Merton. Here destruction and creation, past and present, life and death are one. Here is the kingdom of change, the unchanging. Here a person may stand on Earth and catch a glimpse of eternity, which is—as a wandering carpenter once predicted, and with the confidence of someone who has seen it—an immensely calm and beautiful place.

II.

The national parks and monuments of the Colorado Plateau need your help, in ways both large and small. On the small end are the obvious points—never take home a piece, however small, of Petrified Forest National Park and never disturb even the most inconspicuous fragment of a cliff dwelling. Always scrupulously adhere to park and monument regulations, and be considerate of others on the road, in the campground, and on the trail. When photographing wildlife, always maintain a respectful distance. In a phrase, use common sense.

The larger concerns involve the federal lands in a regional and national context. The public lands on the Colorado Plateau are threatened regionally on several fronts. One Western movement, for example, seeks to nullify federal ownership of public lands by challenging the treaties and agreements by which we (the American people) own the land. This group includes radical members who have bombed federal offices and attempted to kill federal officials. Needless to say, this is a movement (referred to sometimes as the "Sagebrush Rebellion") not to be taken lightly—support federal law enforcement and the rule of law. Nationally, the parks and monuments are imperiled by deep budget cuts and by legislation intended to defund specific units (as happened in 1995 when a bill in the House of Representatives proposed shutting down Hovenweep National Monument). During the period from 1994 to 1997 the Park Service budget shrank by $130 million and the staff was cut from nearly 42,000 to 38,333. The parks and monuments need all the support they can get in both the legislative and executive branches of our federal government.

If you want to be kept abreast of these and other important developments, let me suggest two subscriptions: *Southern Utah Wilderness Alliance* (1471 South 1100, Salt Lake City, Utah 84105, 202-546-2215 and 801-486-3161) and *High Country News* (Post Office Box 1090, Paonia, Colorado 81428, 800-905-1155).

Bryce Overlook, Bryce Canyon National Park

Above all, of course, vote responsibly.

It seems to me after some reflection out there on the desert that five steps would improve the parks and monuments of the Colorado Plateau. My "Modest Proposal" is as follows:

1. Begin restricting the number of people allowed into certain parks or certain parts of parks on a daily basis, as is already done successfully, for example, at such locations as Cumberland Island National Seashore, in Yosemite Valley in Yosemite National Park, and at Brooks Camp in Katmai National Park.

2. Restrict further commercial development in the parks and monuments, and in surrounding national forests and BLM land; it was President Theodore Roosevelt himself who said at the Grand Canyon in 1903:

> *I was delighted to learn of the wisdom of the Santa Fe Railroad in deciding not to build their hotel on the brink of the canyon. I hope you will not have a building of any kind, not a summer cottage, a hotel or anything else, to mar the wonderful grandeur, sublimity, the great loneliness of the canyon. Leave it as it is. You cannot improve on it; not a bit. The ages have been at work on it, and man can only mar it.*

3. Increase concessionaire franchise fees and increase competition for these lucrative contracts, as well as make certain concession fees go directly to the parks and monuments, rather than disappearing into the U.S. Treasury.

4. Rather than continually raising entrance fees (when I was a child, all national parks and monuments were, like libraries and other public institutions, free), begin using monies from the Land and Water Conservation Fund, which generates revenue from federal oil and gas leases. Although this fund has a current balance in excess of $10 billion, and generates additional income every year, Congress has, for some time, been diverting that money for other uses, such as making the federal deficit appear smaller. Releasing the

LWCF funds would do two things: It would bring Congress into compliance with the law it originally passed, and it would bring adequate funding to the parks and monuments that over 200 million Americans use each year.

5. Instead of considering which parks or monuments we should shut down, we should be looking at how to enlarge parks to conform with their ecosystem boundaries and also at which other parts of the public domain might benefit from being granted national park or monument status. We should also be using the LWCF to purchase park inholdings or land around the parks that pose environmental conflicts. The longer we wait, the more expensive these purchases will be.

A vast, free, and well-cared-for public domain is one of the cornerstones of American democracy. These proposals are offered in that spirit.

III.

The Colorado Plateau is many things. It is a desert where all that is not light is stone, and the sun is the color of a newly sliced orange. It is a blue mountain range that has faded into the blue of the sky, so that patches of snow hang like clouds. It is a desert tortoise sleeping comfortably in an old fox den as the temperatures on the coral pink sand dunes above soar to 115 degrees. It is a mountain lion crouched like a shadow near a moonlit pothole at the base of Navajo Mountain, waiting for the deer to pass by. It is the roar of the wind in the ponderosas at Point Sublime, and the thunder of the rapids in Granite Gorge. It is a handpainted hunting scene on a rock panel in Canyonlands National Park that no one has seen in 700 years, and the Ansel Adams photograph of the Temple of the Sun hanging in a crowded gallery at the Metropolitan Museum of Art. It is a wide-eyed little girl from Tokyo seeing the Grand Canyon for the first time, and an elderly couple from Indiana seeing it for the last time.

Sunset on the South Rim, Grand Canyon National Park

In the Middle Ages the faithful, at least once in life, made the pilgrimage to Canterbury, where they beheld the most beautiful cathedral in the land. In our time, we have the Colorado Plateau.

In the end, the Colorado Plateau is more than a place to relax and re-create, to indulge the desires and pursue the idle whim. It is a place to embrace a greater world than our own. The Greeks believed, in one of their familiar paradoxes, that the more responsibilities we assume, the freer we become. One of the lessons of the Colorado Plateau is that we must not leave it behind when we depart. We must do what we can to preserve that which has been so wonderful for us. The Plateau, after all, has given us something more than a few days away from that other world. It has restored our understanding, our equanimity, and our faith. The least we can do, as did the medieval knights of old, is to become sworn defenders of that which has saved us.

PHOTOGRAPHY ON THE

COLORADO PLATEAU

❖

I support a positive philosophy of life and art.

Wherever this leads me, I am sure it is further than were

I a practicing pessimist! I frankly profess a somewhat mystical

concept of nature; I believe the world is incomprehensibly

beautiful—an endless prospect of magic and wonder.

ANSEL ADAMS, Commencement Address, Occidental College (1961)

Most everyone who visits the Colorado Plateau carries a camera. Many dream of taking the perfect photograph. Most do not. Some give up. Others try for years with varying degrees of success. Almost all would benefit from a little practical instruction. I know I would have, twenty-five years ago, when I began photographing nature—how I wish I would have taken one of those courses advertised in the back pages of *Outdoor Photographer* or on the national park bulletin boards. As it turned out, I learned the hard way—through trial and error, with many a wasted roll of film. The purpose of this section is to provide some basic guidance to, hopefully, shorten the learning period. As a former teacher I know that some things that are taught need to be unlearned, and other things that are taught need to be remembered. These are of the latter group.

First of all, you will be photographing in a visually remarkable place: Views extend to the horizons or to the center of the earth, fantastically sculpted rock formations abound, powerful storms form and dissipate even as you watch. Everywhere stark features awaken a sense of the sacred. All this provides you with a distinct advantage over a photographer working in a more mundane setting. Simply having spectacular scenery, however, is not enough—you must avoid the overexposed or underexposed image, the image with insufficient depth of field, the fuzzy image shot from a handheld camera, the poorly composed image, or, worst of all, the cliché image (as in the one-millionth photograph of the Delicate Arch with Mount Tukunikivats framed behind in perfect symmetry).

An ideal photograph for the Colorado Plateau is one that captures the essence of the area: the boundless perspective of space and time, the striking interplay of rock and sky, the combined effect of contemplative peace and penetrating vision. The ideal image (i.e.,

Juniper at sunset, Canyonlands National Park

one you would not be ashamed to frame) should not be so much a recording as a revelation. All the finest photographs of this type— Timothy O'Sullivan's famous 1873 view of the White House Ruins in Canyon de Chelly (can be seen in Goetzmann's *Exploration & Empire;* see Further Reading), Ansel Adams's 1944 color photograph of aspen on the Kaibab Plateau (can be seen in Francos Leydet's *The Grand Canyon: Time and the River Flowing;* see Further Reading)—starkly express the rich mixture of spirit and matter that defines the human experience of the Colorado Plateau.

There are several technical points to be remembered when photographing the desert.

First, the intensity of sunlight is such that a polarizing filter should be used in most situations. This will eliminate much of the atmospheric glare, darken and hence deepen the sky, and enable the lens to penetrate the bottom of shallow canyon streams and pools.

Second, it is easy in the desert to be overwhelmed with a view that extends to the horizon. Use a framing card to isolate your most interesting subjects and try to locate something in the foreground that will make the scene more intimate—a bed of wildflowers, a deer skull or shed antler, a weathered rock formation.

Third, wind is a common problem, especially later in the day. Generally, convectional wind—that caused by warming air—will be less intense earlier in the day, but a passing front can occur at any time and will bring fairly relentless winds, especially on the leading edge of a storm. Carry the heaviest tripod you can, or be prepared to use a rock or the ground to brace the camera, if you are operating, as you should, at the smallest aperture opening possible. Some photographers (see Larry Ulrich's *Wildflowers of the Plateau & Canyon* in Further Reading) use a wind shield to hold wildflowers steady as they strive for maximum depth of field, which means slower shutter speeds.

Fourth, remember the power of the sky—by early afternoon in the summer cumulus clouds will often tower over desert rock formations and distant peaks, creating epic visual effects. I strongly suggest you examine the book about artist Ed Mell, *Beyond the Visible Terrain,* by Donald J. Hagerty (Northland Publishing; see Further Reading)—Mell is a successful Southwestern artist who frequently incorporates dramatic clouds in-to his oil paintings.

Fifth, although the temptation will be to use a wide-angle lens, don't forget that normal, macro, and telephoto lenses can be used to achieve pleasing effects. Telephoto lenses can be used to compress distance and find abstract patterns. Similarly, macro lenses can reveal the often startling beauty of rock surfaces and miniature desert wildflowers.

A few final tips, of the "minor" category: As a general rule, it is advisable to use a 50 or 100 speed film (I use Fuji Velvia/50 speed, or Kodachrome/64 speed). Use a tripod at all times and set your aperture for maximum depth of field (at the risk of repeating myself). Study the light and shoot with your back to the sun whenever possible. Always bracket what you think will be your best photographs—take them at different exposures around what your camera or hand meter tells you is perfect, which may be slightly wrong. Experiment with placing people in your photographs at various distances to provide a sense of scale. In order to develop a sense of artistic composition, study the work of the masters (Ansel Adams, Eliot Porter, and company), visit art museums (art is art, whether photography or oil painting), and over time try to develop your own style which both incorporates and transcends the influences of those you admire. Above all, strive for originality.

The images you return with from the Colorado Plateau will bring happiness for years to come. The deserts are a place for communion and renewal, as well as for artistic expression. In striving for a creative interaction with the landscape, you are joining a tradition that started over a thousand years ago when the Anasazi decorated rock panels with their realistic representations and abstract designs. Sometimes, in photographing their cliff dwellings or rock art, I can almost feel them standing beside me, appraising my work by the standards of excellence they set—brothers and sisters in the oldest guild.

SUGGESTED FIELD EXERCISES

1. Seek out a resonant "deep image" for a particular landscape, a striking photograph that captures the essence of the area. Plan not to take a large volume of photographs but to take several carefully considered exposures at the one location whose vantage best expresses the character of the region. Study maps, talk to rangers or outfitters, and confer with other photographers. Consider how photographers whom you admire might have approached this assignment. Aim

Weathered sandstone along Paria River,
Grand Staircase-Escalante National Monument

not for the standard or cliché scene but for a view of the landscape that has not been recorded before and will forever evoke the surrounding country. Suggestions: (a) The Confluence Trail in Canyonlands National Park will take you into some classic canyonlands country. (b) The alternative trail to Delicate Arch leads through the valley below and provides some unique vantages on the formation. (c) The Bright Angel Trail on the North Rim of the Grand Canyon offers a quick descent into the canyon and some stunning views.

2. Look for unusual shapes and/or patterns on the Colorado Plateau. Quite often, in landscape photography, we find that these patterns—repetitive shapes or designs—are most evident when the sun is low in the sky (sunrise and sunset). Another approach to this assignment would be to use the macro lens and focus on objects at a smaller scale—such as tree bark, bird feathers, or the striated patterns on a piece of sedimentary rock. Suggestions: (a) Just south of the BLM ranger station near Big Water, Arizona, you will find the Paria River trailhead (see Grand Staircase-Escalante National Monument); several miles down the trail are some fantastic formations of cross-bedded sandstone. (b) A telephoto lens will bring the walls of the

Grand Canyon into closer perspective, providing fine views of their patterns. (c) The quaking aspen on the Kaibab Plateau often grow in immaculate groves with perfectly straight, white trunks.

3. Create a photo essay on a particular color in the Colorado Plateau. Red would be a natural choice, with the color common in the sunrises and sunsets, in the spring blossoms of the claret cup and hedgehog cactuses, in the autumnal colors of the fireweed in the Henry Mountains, in the blood-engorged velvet antlers of the deer, and, of course, in various sandstone formations. The possibilities for such a thematic treatment of color in nature are endless, and one could spend months, even years, in completing such a delightful project.

4. Create a photographic portfolio of an animal species. Observe the animal in all four seasons and through the full range of behavioral activities: feeding, playing, breeding, interacting with other species, raising young, old age, and so on. Document the natural history of the animal photographically. Aim for artistic expression as well as for biological precision. What does the study of the animal teach you about the nature of life in a more abstract sense? Are there particular environmental threats to the species? Can you think of outlets in which to publish or display your photographs (ranging from the local newspaper to a national wildlife magazine)? Suggested species: mule deer (North Rim of the Grand Canyon), elk (South Rim of the Grand Canyon), prairie dogs (Canyonlands National Park), golden eagles (Grand Canyon). Years ago, I studied the grizzly bears of Denali National Park. After working six summers and building a portfolio of photographs, I published them as part of an illustrated field guide—one of the most rewarding undertakings of my life.

5. Choose an abstract theme like death and give life to it by assembling a series of moving photographs. In the Grand Canyon, for example, this could include images of the aftermath of the 1996 Bridger's Knoll forest fire, the shed antlers of an elk, the skull of a winter-killed deer, the fallen leaves of a cottonwood among the

river cobblestones, and so forth. One might consider working in black-and-white for such an assignment, the monochromatic treatment further accentuating the theme; conversely, a color presentation could demonstrate how life is part of death, with, for example, bright images of fireweed growing up through the freshly burned trees of the forest fire.

6. In terms of selling your work, you might consider the following: (a) Seek a mentor, someone in your part of the country who is an acknowledged master of landscape or wildlife photography. Study that person's work wherever it is found—illustrated books, periodical articles, museum, or fine art galleries. Befriend this individual. In my case, the photographer was Michio Hoshino, a native of Japan who worked extensively in the wilds of Alaska (until he was killed by a grizzly bear in 1996). I had the chance to shoot beside Michio on a regular basis during the six summers I worked in Denali National Park. Whereas most Western (non-Asian) photographers tried to "fill the frame" when photographing wildlife, Michio's

Courthouse Wash, Arches National Park

technique was completely the opposite—he drew back and shot with a 70 mm or 100 mm while others were using a 300 mm lens. His photographs placed the animal in its world and revealed more than an image that might as well have been taken in a captive situation because of the narrowness of the focus. Needless to say, my study of his approach to nature thoroughly revolutionized my own. (b) Find out what towns in your region offer summer arts festivals. These can provide an excellent opportunity to sell your work, either matted or framed, and to network and build friendships with other photographers. (c) Arrange a meeting with the photo editor of your local newspaper—see if he or she would be interested in a photo essay on the Colorado Plateau, either in the weekly travel section or in the Sunday magazine section.

SUGGESTED TRIPS AND SCENIC DRIVES

❖

Most trips fall in one of three categories—a long weekend (three or four days), an extended weekend trip (five or six days), and a full week trip (seven or more days). There are a variety of beautiful sights and exciting activities that can be packed into any of these time frames. When encountering a new area like the Colorado Plateau, the numerous possibilities can be a bit overwhelming. This section is designed to offer some helpful ideas as you plan your trip. Throughout the Colorado Plateau, the driving distances are quite large. For a trip from my home in Denver to the Grand Canyon, for example, I generally allow a minimum of twelve days (four travel days and eight days in the area for hiking and photography). Careful planning can ensure that your trip is all you hope it will be.

SOUTHERN UTAH

Three Days

I will assume you are entering the region via Interstate 70, having originated either to the east in the Denver area or to the west in the Salt Lake City area. *Day One*—Arrive at noon, drive through Arches National Park (afternoon) and hike to Delicate Arch (3 miles round-trip); *Day Two*—Drive south about 90 miles (total) on U.S. 191 and on State Route 11 to the Needles District of Canyonlands National Park and hike the Confluence Trail (10 miles round-trip); *Day Three*—Drive south about 100 miles on U.S. 191 and State Route 95 to Natural Bridges National Monument and hike to the Owachomo Bridge (.5 mile round-trip), drive north to Interstate 70 and home.

Five Days

Day One—Arrive in Moab area, drive to the Island in the Sky District at Canyonlands National Park and thoroughly explore; *Day Two*—take the scenic drive through Arches National Park, hike to Delicate Arch and to all of the major arches at the end of the road; *Day Three*—Proceed south on U.S. 191 and State Route 12 (total distance of about 90 miles) to the Needles District of Canyonlands National Park and hike the trail to Chesler Park (12 miles round-trip); *Day Four*—Drive south and spend the morning at Natural Bridges National Monument, hiking to one of the three bridges; spend the afternoon at Monument Valley Navajo Tribal Park; *Day Five*—Drive north to Hovenweep National Monument and take the short canyon rim hike; return home.

Seven Days

For this trip, let us assume you enter the region from Interstate 70 in the vicinity of St. George. *Day One*—Spend your first day in Zion National Park, hiking at least several trails in the Zion Canyon central area (such as Upper Emerald Falls and the Riverside Walk at the end of the road); *Day Two*—Drive 80 miles north on U.S. 89 to Bryce Canyon National Park; hike the Queen's Valley Trail and take in the viewpoints (especially Bryce Point); *Day Three*—Drive 50 miles east on State Route 12 to Escalante, stop at the Grand Staircase-Escalante National Monument visitor's center, and, depending on the season, take a medium-length hike; *Day Four*—Proceed north on State Route 12 for about 80 miles to Capitol Reef National Park and drive the scenic route south of the visitor's center; *Day Five*—Proceed to Moab via State Route 24 and Interstate 70 (a total distance of around 150 miles, or 2.5 hours driving time) and explore the Island in the Sky District of Canyonlands National Park north of Moab; *Day Six*—Drive the park road at Arches National Park and hike the trail to Delicate Arch; *Day Seven*—Explore some of the arches at the end of the park in the early morning; proceed north to Interstate 70 and drive home in the afternoon.

NORTHERN ARIZONA

Three Days

I will assume your trip begins at Flagstaff, on Interstate 40, and that you arrive from Albuquerque to the east, Las Vegas to the west, or Phoenix to the south. *Day One*—proceed north of Flagstaff for 80 miles on U.S. 180 to the South Rim of the Grand Canyon; spend an hour orienting at the visitor's center and the rim; walk along the West Rim in the afternoon; *Day Two*—hike down a couple of miles on one of the popular South Rim trails (such as Bright Angel); *Day Three*—Proceed east out of the park on State Route 64; at the junction with U.S. 89 turn south and spend the morning visiting Wupatki National Monument and Sunset Crater National Monument before returning to Interstate 40 and the drive home.

Five Days

I will assume your route of entry is from Flagstaff. *Day One*—Arrive at the South Rim of the Grand Canyon via U.S. 180 about 80 miles north of Flagstaff; spend some time at the visitor's center and proceed to the backcountry office near park headquarters to secure a permit for two nights in the canyon; *Day Two*—Hike into the canyon to your first night's campsite, explore the country; *Day Three*—Hike to your second night's campsite, explore the country; *Day Four*—Hike out of the canyon, take time to rest; *Day Five*—Proceed east out of the park on State Route 64; at the junction with U.S. 89 turn south and spend the morning visiting Wupatki National Monument and Sunset Crater National Monument before returning to Interstate 70 and the drive home.

Seven Days

I will assume you are entering northern Arizona from U.S. 160 south of Durango, a popular route for people from Front Range Colorado. *Day One*—Drive through Four Corners to the junction with U.S. 191; turn south and drive to Canyon de Chelly National Monument (about 90 miles from Four Corners); spend the afternoon hiking to and exploring the White House Ruins (trail is 3 miles round-trip down into a canyon); *Day Two*—Continue south on U.S. 191 for 70 miles to Interstate 40; drive west to Painted Desert National Park and spend the day exploring; *Day Three*—After spending the night in the environs of Flagstaff, proceed north to the Grand Canyon on U.S. 180 (about 80 miles); familiarize yourself with the park at the visitor's center; walk the trail along the West Rim; *Day Four*—Hike a couple of miles into the canyon on one of the popular trails; *Day Five*—Visit the Desert View area about 20 miles east of Grand Canyon Village; stop at the viewpoints; *Day Six*—Drive east out of the park on State Route 64 and turn north at the junction with U.S. 89 (total distance about 80 miles from Desert View) and drive to Page; spend the afternoon on a half-day tour of Lake Powell; *Day Seven*—Drive back toward Four Corners via U.S. 89 and U.S. 160, stopping for a visit in Monument Valley Navajo Tribal Park.

WESTERN COLORADO AND NORTHWESTERN NEW MEXICO

Three Days

I will assume you are arriving on Interstate 70 in the vicinity of Grand Junction, Colorado. *Day One*—Just west of Grand Junction exit at Fruita and spend the day driving through and exploring

Colorado National Monument. *Day Two*—Drive north of Grand Junction on State Route 139 for 63 miles; at Rangeley turn north on State Route 64 and drive about 20 miles to U.S. 40; take the park road to Echo Park and spend the day exploring the river canyon; *Day Three*—Drive to the Dinosaur Fossil Quarry and spend the day exploring; return to Grand Junction and home.

Five Days

I will assume you are beginning on U.S. 160 near Durango, Colorado. *Day One*—Drive west of town on U.S. 160 for about 40 miles to Mesa Verde National Park; spend the afternoon exploring the ruins at Chapin Mesa; *Day Two*—Explore the ruins on Wetherill Mesa in Mesa Verde; *Day Three*—Drive south on U.S. 160 through Shiprock and U.S. 64 (turn east); at Bloomfield turn south on State Route 44 to Chaco Culture National Historical Park (total distance from Mesa Verde about 180 miles); *Day Four*—Further explore the ruins at Chaco; *Day Five*—Return north on State Route 44, stopping at Aztec Ruins National Monument just north of Aztec.

FOUR CORNERS

Seven Days

This trip involves destinations in all four states. *Day One*—Along Interstate 40 west of Albuquerque, spend the morning visiting Acoma Pueblo and spend the afternoon at El Malpais and El Morro National Monuments; spend the night in Gallup, 139 miles west of Albuquerque; *Day Two*—Drive west about 50 miles to U.S. 191 in Arizona; turn north and visit Hubbell Trading Post National Historical Site (37 miles north) and Canyon de Chelly National Monument (another 35 miles north); *Day Three*—Continue exploring Canyon de Chelly; *Day Four*—Drive north on U.S. 191 to the junction with U.S. 160; turn west to Kayenta and then drive north on U.S. 163 to Monument Valley Navajo Tribal Park; spend the afternoon exploring the park (total driving distance of around 120 miles); *Day Five*—Return to Four Corners via U.S. 163 and U.S. 160 and spend the afternoon at Mesa Verde National Park (total driving distance of around 130 miles); *Day Six*—Continue exploring Mesa Verde National Park; *Day Seven*—Return south via U.S. 550 and State Route 44 to Interstate 40, stopping at Chaco Culture National Historic Park if time permits (total distance of around 180 miles or 3 hours of driving time).

PRACTICAL INFORMATION

❖

HOTEL & MOTEL CHAINS

Best Western—(800) 528-1234
Comfort Inn—(800) 228-5150
Day's Inn—(800) 329-7466
Holiday Inn—(800) HOLIDAY
Quality Inn—(800) 221-2222
Ramada Inn—(800) HOTELS-1
Super 8—(800) 800-8000
TraveLodge—(800) 578-7878

GENERAL INFORMATION

Arizona Office of Tourism—1100 West Washington Street,
    Phoenix, Arizona 85007; (800) 842-8257, (602) 542-8687.
Arizona State Parks Office—1300 West Washington, Suite 104,
    Phoenix, Arizona 85007; (602) 542-4174.

Bureau of Land Management—435 North Main, Post Office Box 7, Monticello, Utah 84535; (801) 587-2141.

Colorado Parks and Outdoor Recreation—1313 Sherman Street, Room 618, Denver Colorado 80203; (303) 866-3437.

Colorado Tourism Bureau—1677 Wadsworth Boulevard, Lakewood, Colorado 80202; (303) 232-1500, (800) 608-4748.

New Mexico Department of Tourism—Lamy Building, Room 106, 491 Old Santa Fe Trail, Santa Fe, New Mexico 87503; (505) 827-7400, (800) 545-2040.

New Mexico State Parks—408 Galisteo Street, Santa Fe, New Mexico 87504; (505) 827-7465.

U.S. Forest Service for Colorado—740 Simms, Lakewood, Colorado 80225; (303) 275-5350, (800) 280-Camp.

U.S. Forest Service for the Southwest—Public Affairs Office, USFS, Southwestern Region, 517 Gold Avenue, Albuquerque, New Mexico 87102; (800) 280-CAMP, (505) 842-3292.

Utah Campground Owners Association—1370 W. North Temple, Salt Lake City, Utah 84116; (801) 521-2582.

Utah Convention and Visitors Bureau—180 S. West Temple, Salt Lake City, Utah 84101; (801) 521-2822.

Utah Division of Parks and Recreation—1636 W. North Temple, Salt Lake City, Utah 84116; (801) 538-7221, (800) 322-3770.

Utah Division of Wildlife Resources—15 W. North Temple, Salt Lake City, Utah 84116; (801) 528-4700 (fishing and hunting x8660; birdline x4887).

Utah Travel Council—Council Hall, Salt Lake City, Utah 84114; (801) 538-1030 (maps, travel publications, bed and breakfast information, all available free).

SOUTHERN UTAH

Arches National Park

Arches National Park—Superintendent, Post Office Box 907, Moab, Utah 84532-0907; (801) 259-8161/5279.

Lin Ottinger's Scenic Tours—Moab Rock Shop, 600 North Main, Moab, Utah 84532; (801) 259-7312 (guided four-wheel-drive tours of Canyonlands; superb rock and fossil shop).

Pack Creek Ranch—Box 1270, Moab, Utah 84532; (801) 259-5505 (cabins and horseback rides in the area around Moab).

Bryce Canyon National Park

Bryce Canyon National Park—Superintendent, Bryce Canyon, Utah 84717-0001; (801) 834-5322.

Best Western Ruby's Inn—Bryce Canyon, Utah 84717-0001; (801) 834-5341 (1 mile north of park entrance, features ski touring and snowmobiling in the winter, helicopter rides and rodeos in the summer).

Bryce Canyon Lodge—Bryce Canyon, Utah 84717-0001; (801) 834-5361 (inside the park, built for the Union Pacific in the 1920s, with much charm, open mid-April through October).

Canyon Trail Rides, Incorporated—Box 128, Tropic, Utah 84776; (801) 834-5219 (trail rides in the park).

Canyonlands National Park

Canyonlands National Park—Superintendent, 2282 S. West Resource Boulevard, Moab, Utah 84532-8000; (801) 259-7164.

Adrift Adventures—Box 577, Moab, Utah 84532; (800) 874-4483, (801) 259-8594 (four-wheel-drive tours and rafting trips).

Needles Outpost—Box 1107, Monticello, Utah 84535; (801) 259-2032/8545 (restaurant with excellent black bean burritos, general store, on-site camping, four-wheel-drive trips, and scenic aerial tours).

Redtail Aviation—Box 515, Moab, Utah 84532; (801) 259-7421/3412 (aerial tours over the park).

Capitol Reef National Park

Capitol Reef National Park—Superintendent, HC 70 Box 15, Torrey, Utah 84775-9602; (801) 425-3791.

Best Western Capitol Reef Resort—Torrey, Utah 84775-9602;
(801) 425-3761 (near the park entrance).

Rim Rock Resort Ranch—General Delivery, Utah 24, Torrey, Utah
84775-9602; (801) 425-3843 (offers horseback riding).

Cedar Breaks National Monument

Cedar Breaks National Monument—Superintendent, 82 North 100
East Street, Cedar City, Utah 84702-2606; (801) 586-9451.

Abbey's Inn—940 West 200 North, Cedar City, Utah 84702-2606;
(801) 586-9966 (indoor swimming pool).

Best Western Town & Country Inn—200 North Main, Cedar City,
Utah 84702-2606; (801) 586-9900 (nice gift shop).

Glen Canyon National Recreation Area

Glen Canyon National Recreation Area—Superintendent, Post
Office Box 1507, Page, Arizona, 86040-1507; (520) 608-6404.

Halls Crossing Marine—Lake Powell, Utah 84533; (801) 684-2261,
(800) 528-6154 (boat tours of Lake Powell).

Lake Powell Air Service—Box 1385, Page, Arizona 86040-0035;
(602) 645-2494, (800) 245-8688 (guided aerial tours over
Glen Canyon).

Lake Powell Tours—Box 40, St. George, Utah 84770; (801) 673-
1733 (boat tours of Lake Powell).

Wahweap Lodge and Marina—Box 1597, Page, Arizona 86040;
(602) 645-2433, (800) 528-6154 (tours of Lake Powell).

Grand Staircase - Escalante National Monument

Grand Staircase-Escalante National Monument—Superintendent,
Post Office Box 225, Escalante, Utah 84726, (801) 826-4291;
information also available at BLM Kanab Resource Area Office,
318 North First East, Kanab, Utah 84741, (801) 644-2672.

Escalante Canyon Outfitters—Post Office Box 1330, Boulder, Utah
84716; (801) 335-7311, 888-ECO-HIKE (a husband and wife
with long experience in the new national monument who

provide guided backpack and horse pack trips into the area—
highly recommended).

Hovenweep National Monument
Hovenweep National Monument—Superintendent, McElmo Route,
    Cortez, Colorado 81321-8901; (970) 529-4461.

Natural Bridges National Monument
Natural Bridges National Monument—Superintendent, Post Office
    Box 1, Lake Powell, Utah 84533-0001; (801) 692-1234.
Grayson Country Inn, 118 E. 300 South, Blanding, Utah 84500;
    (801) 678-2388 (seven guest rooms).

Rainbow Bridge National Monument
Rainbow Bridge National Monument—c/o Glen Canyon National
    Recreation Area, Post Office Box 1507, Page, Arizona
    86040-1507; (520) 645-2511.
Bullfrog Resort and Marina—Box 4055, Lake Powell, Arizona
    84533; (801) 684-2233, (800) 528-6154 (one-day boat trips to
    the monument).

Zion National Park
Zion National Park—Superintendent, Springdale, Utah
    84767-1099; (801) 772-3256.
Canyon Trail Rides, Incorporated—Box 128, Tropic, Utah 84776;
    (801) 772-3967 (trail rides in the park).
Day's Inn & Four Seasons Convention Center—747 East St. George
    Boulevard, St. George, Utah 84750; (801) 673-6111 (palm trees,
    swimming pool, tennis courts).
Kanab Air Service—2378 S 175 East 125th, Kanab, Utah 84741;
    (801) 644-2904 (scenic flights).
Flanagan's Inn—428 Zion Park Boulevard, Springdale, Utah 84767;
    (801) 772-3244, (800) 765-7787.
Zion Lodge—Zion National Park, Springdale, Utah 84767;
    (801) 586-7687 (only lodging available in the park).

Canyon de Chelly National Monument

Canyon de Chelly National Monument—Superintendent, Post Office Box 588, Chinle, Arizona 86503-0588; (520) 675-5500.

Thunderbird Lodge Tours—Box 548, Chinle, Arizona 86503; (520) 674-5842 (tours to remote areas of the monument requiring Indian guides).

Grand Canyon National Park

Grand Canyon National Park—Superintendent, Post Office Box 128, Grand Canyon, Arizona 86023-0129; (520) 638-7888.

Backcountry Permits—Backcountry Office, Grand Canyon National Park, Post Office Box 128, Grand Canyon, Arizona 86023.

Camping—DESTINET, Post Office Box 85705, San Diego, California 92186-5705; Mather Campground at South Rim— (800) 365-2267; RV trailers at Trailer Village on the South Rim—(303) 297-2757.

Grand Canyon Airlines—Box 3038, Grand Canyon, Arizona 86023; (520) 638-2407, (800) 528-2413 (scenic flights).

Grand Canyon Dories—Box 215, Altaville, California 95221; (209) 736-0805 (extended dory and raft trips down the Colorado and San Juan Rivers).

Grand Canyon Expeditions Company—Box O, Kanab, Utah 84741; (800) 544-2691 (week- and two-week-long trips down the Colorado).

Grand Canyon Field Institute—P.O. 399, Grand Canyon, Arizona 86023; (520) 638-2485.

Grand Canyon Trip Planners—TRIP PLANNER, Post Office Box 129, Grand Canyon, Arizona 86023.

Havasupai Tourist Enterprises—Supai, Arizona 86435; (520) 448-2121 (overnight trips into Havasupai Canyon).

Jacob Lake Gas Station (mechanic)—U.S. 89 & State Route 67, Jacob Lake, Arizona 86022; (520) 643-7232.

Jacob Lake Inn and Country Store—U.S. 89 & State Route 67, Jacob Lake, Arizona 86022; (520) 526-0924.

Jacob Lake RV Park—U.S. 89 & State Route 67, Jacob Lake, Arizona 86022; (520) 628-8851.

Kaibab National Forest—Supervisor's Office, 800 South 6th Street, Williams, Arizona 86046; (520) 635-2681.

Kaibab Plateau Visitor Center—U.S. 89 & State Route 67, Jacob Lake, Arizona 86022; (520) 643-7298.

North Kaibab Ranger District—Post Office Box 248, Fredonia, Arizona 86022; (520) 635-2681.

North Rim Lodge—(520) 638-2611.

North Rim Mule Trips—summer (520) 638-2292; winter (801) 679-8665.

South Rim Lodge—Amfac Parks and Resorts, 14001 East Iliff, Aurora, Colorado 80041; (303) 297-2757.

South Rim Mule Trips—Bright Angel Transportation Desk; (303) 297-2757.

Hubbell Trading Post National Historical Site

Hubbell Trading Post National Historical Site—Post Office Box 150, Ganado, Arizona 86505-0150; (520) 755-3475.

Montezuma Castle National Monument

Montezuma Castle National Monument—Superintendent, Post Office Box 219, Camp Verde, Arizona 86322-0219; (520) 567-3322.

Monument Valley Navajo Tribal Park

Monument Valley Navajo Tribal Park—Superintendent, Post Office Box 360289, Monument Valley, Utah 84536; (801) 727-3353/3287, or Navajo Parks and Recreation Department, Post Office Box 308, Window Rock, Arizona

86515; (520) 871-4941, extension 6647 [commercial
photography requires a permit—contact Department of
Broadcast Service, Post Office Box 308, Window Rock, Arizona
86515; or phone (520) 871-6656 or (520) 871-6555].

Crawley's Monument Valley Tours—Box 187, Kayenta, Arizona
86033; (520) 697-3463 (tours of Monument Valley and other
nearby areas).

Goulding's Monument Valley Tours—Box 1, Monument Valley,
Utah 84536; (800) 874-0902, (801) 727-3231,
fax (801) 727-3344 (restaurant, grocery store, gift shop,
gas station, and motel).

Recapture Lodge Tours—Box 309, Bluff, Utah 84512;
(801) 672-2281 (guided four-wheel-drive tours of Monument
Valley and nearby areas).

Navajo National Monument

Navajo National Monument—Superintendent, HC 71, Box 3,
Tonalea, Arizona 86044-9704; (520) 672-2366.

Navajo National Monument Backpacking and Rides—Navajo
National Monument, HC 71, Box 3, Tonalea Arizona 86044-
9704; (520) 672-2366 (rides to the more remote Keet Seel Ruins
from Memorial Day through Labor Day).

Pipe Spring National Monument

Pipe Spring National Monument—Superintendent, HC 65 Box 5,
Fredonia, Arizona 86022-9600; (520) 643-7105.

Sunset Crater Volcano National Monument

Sunset Crater Volcano National Monument—Superintendent,
Route 3 Box 149, Flagstaff, Arizona 86004-9420;
(520) 556-7042.

Walnut Canyon National Monument

Walnut Canyon National Monument—Superintendent, Walnut
Canyon Road #3; Flagstaff, Arizona 86004-9705;
(520) 526-3367.

Wupatki National Monument

Wupatki National Monument—Superintendent, HC 33, Box 444A,
Flagstaff, Arizona 86004-9814; (520) 679-2365.

WESTERN COLORADO AND NORTHWESTERN NEW MEXICO

Aztec Ruins National Monument

Aztec Ruins National Monument—Superintendent, Post Office Box
640, Aztec, New Mexico 87410-0640; (505) 334-6174.

Chaco Culture National Historical Park

Chaco Culture National Historical Park—Superintendent, Post
Office Box 220, Nageezi, New Mexico 87307-0220;
(505) 786-7014.

Colorado National Monument

Colorado National Monument—Superintendent, Fruita, Colorado
81521-9530; (970) 858-3617.

Dinosaur National Monument

Dinosaur National Monument—Superintendent, 4545 State Route
40, Dinosaur, Colorado 81610-9724; (970) 374-3000.

El Malpais National Monument

El Malpais National Monument—Superintendent, Post Office Box
939, Grants, New Mexico 87020-0939; (505) 783-4774.

El Morro National Monument

El Morro National Monument—Superintendent, Route 2 Box 43, Ramah, New Mexico 87321-9603; (505) 783-4226.

Mesa Verde National Park

Mesa Verde National Park—Superintendent, Post Office Box 8, Mesa Verde, Colorado 81330-0008; (970) 529-4465.

Strater Hotel—699 Main Street, Durango, Colorado 81320; (970) 259-5373 (nice Victorian).

Yucca House National Monument

Yucca House National Monument—c/o Superintendent, Mesa Verde National Park, Post Office Box 8, Mesa Verde, Colorado 81330-0008; (970) 529-4465.

FURTHER READING

❖

Herewith is what I call the "Slickrock Library," an informal list of indispensable titles on the Colorado Plateau. I own all these books, and so I recommend them from long personal acquaintance, in the same way I would recommend a trusted friend. If someone were to request a "Top Five" list, I would include, in the following order, Abbey's *Desert Solitaire,* for the powerful lyrical writing, strong sense of place, and complete honesty; Major Powell's *The Exploration of the Colorado River and Its Canyons,* for one of the most incredible adventures ever experienced by anyone, anywhere—especially considering the man only had one arm; anything by Clarence Dutton, for the authoritative and eloquent writing on the essential Colorado Plateau subject of geology; John Van Dyke's *The Grand Canyon of the Colorado,* for the sheer passion of the essays; and William Goetzmann's *Exploration & Empire,* for the fascinating human history of the Plateau in its early formative years, written by the reigning academic authority on the subject.

Abbey, Edward. *Abbey's Road.* New York: Dutton, 1979. Vintage
Abbey. This is the book that solidified Abbey's reputation as the
resident bard and guardian spirit of the Colorado Plateau.
Includes essays on Canyonlands National Park, Lake Powell,
and—my favorite—a nowhere place called Cape Solitude on
the south rim of the Grand Canyon.

———. *The Best of Edward Abbey.* San Francisco: Sierra Club,
1984. This is a fine compendium, with vintage essays on
the Plateau from other volumes. If you can afford to own only
two Abbey books, buy this one and *Desert Solitaire* and you'll
have the best. Includes the essay "Down the [Green] River with
Henry Thoreau," on which I published my one and only
scholarly article (Abbey as a writer of jeremiads) in *Western
American Literature.* Also contains "Fire Lookout" about his
life for four seasons on the North Rim of the Grand Canyon.

———. *Beyond the Wall.* New York: Holt, Rinehart and Winston,
1984. Includes the narrative of Abbey's hike with Tom Lyon
down the Paria River (Buckskin Gulch), as well his float trip
through the Grand Canyon with photographer John Blaustein,
which produced the book *The Hidden Canyon,* now out of
print but rumored to be in the mill for a reprint at the
University of California Press.

———. *Desert Solitaire.* New York: McGraw-Hill, 1968. The book
that started it all, at least for me. My mother gave me a copy
back in 1972, when I was eighteen, and after that I just had to
visit the place—the Colorado Plateau, that is. This is Abbey's
masterpiece. The essay "Down the River" relates Abbey's
incredible trip through the lovely lost Glen Canyon before the
dam—he and his friend Ralph Newcomb were among the last
people on Earth to see it.

———. *Down the River.* New York: Dutton, 1982. A great little
book, with fine essays on the San Juan River, the Colorado
River, the Green River, and others.

———. *The Journey Home: Some Words in Defense of the American*

West. New York: Dutton, 1977. Includes his magnificent tribute to the Colorado Plateau entitled "Come on In" as well as "Down the River with Major Powell" (on the Green River) and "The Crooked Woods" (on the North Rim of the Grand Canyon).

————. *One Life at a Time, Please.* New York: Henry Holt, 1988. His last book of essays—he died one year later, at the age of 62. The title comes from the last words spoken by Abbey's philosophical mentor, Thoreau. Includes the account of a week that Abbey spent alone floating the Colorado River a few years before his death.

————. *Slickrock.* With photographs by Philip Hyde. San Francisco: Sierra Club, 1971. This book has recently been reprinted by Gibbs Smith. It features some sublime photographs by Philip Hyde and some nice essays by Abbey, particularly the piece describing his 20-mile hike to Skyline Arch.

Baars, Donald L. *The Colorado Plateau: A Geological History.* Albuquerque: University of New Mexico Press, 1983. A comprehensive summary of the geology of the canyonlands. For sale in the Canyonlands National Park visitor's center.

Banham, Peter Reyner. *Scenes in America Deserta.* Salt Lake City: Gibbs M. Smith, 1982. Some fine essays.

Barnes, F.A. *Canyon Country Prehistoric Rock Art.* Salt Lake City: Wasatch, 1982. One of an extensive (over twenty) series of books by Barnes on the Canyon Country—a thoroughly researched book that also includes a listing of sites in national parks and monuments.

————. *Utah Canyon Country.* Salt Lake City: Utah Geographic Series, 1986. A lavishly illustrated look at the Plateau in Utah— the perfect inexpensive gift book.

Bowden, Charles. *Desierto.* New York: Norton, 1991. Bowden lives on the Sonoran desert—anyone loving deserts will find a kindred spirit at work here.

Doolittle, Jerome. *Canyons and Mesas.* New York: Time-Life Books, 1974. This is one of the magnificent "American Wilderness" books published by Time-Life in the 1970s—a superb title, with photo-essays on Navajo Mountain, Rainbow Bridge, and other sites on the Plateau.

Dutton, Clarence. *Report on the Geology of the High Plateaus of Utah.* Washington, D.C.: U.S. Government, 1880. Not nearly as boring as the title suggests—this and other Dutton works are available in modern reprints.

———. *Tertiary History of the Grand Canon District.* Washington, D.C.: U.S. Government, 1882; Layton, Utah: Peregrine Smith, 1977. Another classic by the master. As with *Report,* this is available as a reprint from Gibbs Smith.

Eddington, Patrick and Susan Makov. *Trading Post Guidebook: Where to Find the Trading Posts, Galleries, Auctions, Artists, and Museums of the Four Corners Region.* Flagstaff: Northland Publishing, 1995. A wonderful guide that covers everything from the pueblos of the upper Rio Grande to the Watchtower at Desert View in Grand Canyon National Park.

Ellis, Reuben, editor. *Stories and Stones: Writing the Anasazi Homeland—An Anthology.* Boulder: Pruett, 1995. Includes writings on Chaco Canyon, Canyon de Chelly, Mesa Verde, and Hovenweep.

Fielder, John. *Colorado BLM Wildlands: A Guide to Hiking & Floating Colorado's Canyon Country.* Denver: Westcliffe, 1994. This is a complete guide to the numerous BLM wild areas on the Colorado Plateau in western Colorado. A similar book could, and should, be written for Utah. Many of these remote areas offer wilderness experiences unlike anything that can be found in the national parks or monuments.

Fletcher, Colin. *The Man Who Walked Through Time.* New York: Knopf, 1968. An incredible tale, and one of the few books published in 1968 destined to still be in print in 2068, or 2168.

Goeztmann, William H. *Exploration & Empire: The Explorer and the Scientist in the Winning of the American West.* New York: Norton,

1967. This book was awarded the Pulitzer prize for history in the year of its publication—need I say more? No one does it better than Goetzmann, who tells us everything about the extraordinary Age of Discovery in the American West.

————. *The West of the Imagination.* New York: Norton, 1986. A companion volume to the 1986 PBS special, with an excellent narrative written by Goetzmann and his son, who was for a time a curator at the Denver Art Museum—wonderful graphics.

Hagerty, Donald J. *Beyond the Visible Terrain: The Art of Ed Mell.* Flagstaff: Northland Publishing, 1996. Great artist!

Harris, Ann and Esther Tuttle. *Geology of the National Parks.* Dubuque, Iowa: Kendall/Hunt Publishing Company, 1990. So far as I know, this is the only book of its sort on its subject. The authors provide a detailed explanation of the geology of the fifty most important national parks in the country. I bought my copy in the visitor's center at Capitol Reef National Park, after considerable debate (it lists for $40). I have used it a hundred times since—an absolutely essential book for all lovers of the national parks.

Inkslip, Eleanor. *The Colorado River Through Glen Canyon Before Lake Powell: Historic Photo Journal, 1872 to 1964.* Moab: Inkslip Books, 1995. A moving photographic chronicle of Glen Canyon before and after the dam.

Jett, Stephen J. *Navajo Wildlands.* With photographs by Philip Hyde. San Francisco: Sierra Club, 1967. Long out of print, but you can still find copies in used bookstores, which is where I obtained my copy. A priceless book—stunning photographs by Philip Hyde, and some excellent essays by both Hyde and the author.

Krutch, Joseph Wood. *The Grand Canyon.* New York: William Sloane, 1958. Krutch moved to the Southwest after his retirement from Columbia University, where he had worked as an English professor. This book includes his essays on the ecology and geology of the canyon.

Larson, Peggy. *The Deserts of the Southwest.* San Francisco: Sierra Club, 1977. Though somewhat dated, this guidebook, part of a series published by Sierra Club twenty years ago, covers the Colorado Plateau as part of the Great Basin desert.

Lavender, Dave. *One Man's West.* Lincoln: University of Nebraska, 1943, 1977. This is the best book ever written on southwestern Colorado, including the canyon country around the Dolores River.

Leydet, François. *The Grand Canyon, Time and the River Flowing.* San Francisco: Sierra Club, 1964. I finally found a copy in a used book store recently, and bought it, despite the price ($100). This is not just a book. It is an incredible work of art, with photographs by Ansel Adams, Eliot Porter, Philip Hyde, and others. It is also one of the now classic large-format books that David Brower published during the 1960s when the battles were raging over the Colorado River system. Because of books like this, we do not have dams in the Grand Canyon, in Dinosaur National Monument, and elsewhere.

Lopez, Barry. *Desert Notes.* New York: Scribner's, 1976. One of Lopez's finest books—a series of meditations on the desert. Although written about the Mojave, the book's sentiments and revelations are relevant to the Painted Desert, or any desert for that matter.

Muir, John. *Steep Trails.* San Francisco: Sierra Club, 1994. Includes Muir's essay "The Grand Canyon of the Colorado."

Oppelt, Norman T. *Guide to Prehistoric Ruins of the Southwest.* Boulder: Pruett Publishing Company, 1981. A handy guide if ruins are your passion.

Patterson, Alex. *A Field Guide to Rock Art Symbols of the Greater Southwest.* Boulder: Johnson Books, 1995. This book is a very useful guide in the field as you encounter these often mysterious pictographs and symbols.

Philips, Arthur M. *Grand Canyon Wildflowers.* Grand Canyon:

Grand Canyon Natural History Association, 1979. A fine illustrated field guide, arranged by color.

Porter, Eliot. *The Place No One Knew: Glen Canyon on the Colorado.* San Francisco: Sierra Club Books, 1963.

Powell, John Wesley. *The Exploration of the Colorado River and Its Canyons.* Washington, D.C.: U.S. Government, 1874; New York: Dover, 1961. Certainly one of the most important books ever written about the Colorado Plateau. Reads like an adventure novel about a modern Ulysses.

Stegner, Wallace. *The American West as Living Space.* Ann Arbor: University of Michigan Press, 1987. More essays on the Colorado Plateau.

———. *Beyond the Hundredth Meridian: John Wesley Powell and the Second Opening of the West.* Boston: Houghton Mifflin, 1954. Stegner contextualizes Powell and the age in which he lived—his political battles, for funding, were sometimes nearly as difficult as his battles with rapids and whirlpools on the Colorado River.

———. *Clarence Dutton: An Appraisal.* Salt Lake City: University of Utah Press, 1936. This was Stegner's doctoral dissertation at the University of Iowa.

———. *The Sound of Mountain Water.* Lincoln: University of Nebraska Press, 1985. Includes such essays as "San Juan and Glen Canyon," "Glen Canyon Submersus," and "Navajo Rodeo."

———. *Where the Bluebird Sings to the Lemonade Springs.* New York: Penguin, 1994. This was Stegner's last book of essays. "Thoughts on a Dry Land" relates strongly to the Colorado Plateau.

Stokes, William Lee. *Geology of Utah.* Salt Lake City: Utah Museum of Natural History, 1987. An indispensable fat reference book covering the geological provinces of the state in great detail.

Ulrich, Larry. *Wildflowers of the Plateau & Canyon.* Santa Barbara: Companion Press, 1995. The *best* book available on the wildflowers of the Colorado Plateau. Not a guide book *per se,* but something much better—fine photographs by a modern master of over 100 Colorado Plateau flowers in their natural setting. Available in the visitor's center at the Grand Canyon and in adjacent stores. A real bargain at $18.95.

Van Dyke, John Charles. *The Desert.* New York: Scribner's, 1901; Layton, Utah: Peregrine Smith, 1908. An examination of the aesthetics of desert appreciation.

———— *The Grand Canyon of the Colorado.* New York: Scribner's, 1920. One of the classic literary works on the Grand Canyon.

Wild, Peter, editor. *The Desert Reader.* Salt Lake City: University of Utah, 1991. A good anthology, with selections by John Wesley Powell, Clarence E. Dutton, John Van Dyke, Joseph Wood Krutch, Edward Abbey, and Wallace Stegner ("The Geography of Hope").

Williams, Terry Tempest. *Pieces of White Shell: A Journey to Navajoland.* New York: Scribner's, 1984. The author roams through Navajo Country, enlarging her view of wild nature and human nature.

————. *Refuge: An Unnatural History of Family and Place.* New York: Pantheon, 1991. An incredibly moving work, one of the few books written in our time that will endure. Chronicles the death of the author's mother to ovarian cancer, and the death of a salt marsh near Salt Lake City.

Zwinger, Ann. *Downcanyon.* Tucson: University of Arizona Press, 1995. Zwinger, an accomplished writer, naturalist, and artist, writes of the Grand Canyon, including a backpacking trip with her daughter (both women over fifty) to the bottom of the canyon and back.

————. *Run, River, Run.* New York: Harper & Row, 1975. The author walks and floats the length of the Green River, analyzing natural history along the way.

————. *Wind in the Rock.* New York: Harper & Row, 1978. Zwinger rambles through the canyons of southern Utah, which abound with cliff dwellings and geological wonders.

INDEX

❖

Page numbers in italics refer to images.

ABOUT THE AUTHOR

John A. Murray was born in Cincinnati, Ohio, on January 27, 1954. He holds degrees in English from the University of Colorado and the University of Denver. From 1988 through 1994 he was an English professor at the University of Alaska, Fairbanks, where he also directed the graduate degree program in professional writing. Murray is the author of over two dozen works of natural history, including *A Republic of Rivers: Three Centuries of Nature Writing from Alaska and the Yukon* (Oxford University Press, 1990), *Out Among the Wolves: Contemporary Writings on the Wolf* (Alaska Northwest, 1993), and *The Sierra Club Nature Writing Handbook* (Sierra Club Books, 1994). In 1995 he was made a life member of the Nature Conservancy. He has been hiking, photographing, and painting the Colorado Plateau since the 1970s. John Murray makes his home in Denver, Colorado.

Other books by John A. Murray include *The Indian Peaks Wilderness* (Pruett Publishing, 1985); *Wildlife in Peril: The Endangered Mammals of Colorado* (Roberts Rinehart, 1987); *The Gila Wilderness* (University of New Mexico, 1988); *The Last Grizzly, and Other Southwestern Bear Stories* [with David Brown] (University of Arizona, 1989); *The South San Juan Wilderness* (Pruett Publishing, 1989); *The Islands and the Sea: Five Centuries of Nature*

Writing from the Caribbean (Oxford University, 1992); *The Great Bear: Contemporary Writings on the Grizzly* (Alaska Northwest, 1992); *Nature's New Voices* (Fulcrum, 1992); *Wild Hunters: Predators in Peril* [with Monte Hummel and Sherri Pettigrew] (Roberts Rinehart, 1992); *Wild Africa: Three Centuries of Nature Writing from Africa* (Oxford University, 1993); *A Thousand Leagues of Blue: The Sierra Club Book of the Pacific* (Sierra Club, 1993); *American Nature Writing 1994* (Sierra Club, 1994); *Grizzly Bears* (Roberts Rinehart, 1995); *American Nature Writing 1995* (Sierra Club, 1995); *The Walker's Companion* [with Dave Wallace, and others] (Time-Life Books, Weldon Owen Publishing, and The Nature Company, 1995); *American Nature Writing 1996* (Sierra Club, 1996); *Cactus Country: The Deserts of the American Southwest* (Roberts Rinehart, 1996); *Alaska* (Compass American Guides/Random House, 1997); *American Nature Writing 1997* (Sierra Club, 1997); *The Colorado Plateau* (Northland Publishing, 1998); *American Nature Writing 1998* (Sierra Club, 1998); and *Rivers* (Lyons & Burford, 1998)